THE POWER OF THE UNSEEN

THE POWER OF THE UNSEEN

Marcel Borgi

ISBN-10: 1517261236
ISBN-13: 9781517261238
Library of Congress Control Number: 2015915034
CreateSpace Independent Publishing Platform
North Charleston, South Carolina

To all the people who have fears and worries, to all the people who are suffering from hunger and mistreatment, to all the people who are not happy with what they have, to all the people who can't see the light in their hearts, to the people who need to love and be loved, to all the sick, and to all the less fortunate.

You can't stop the waves, but you can learn to surf.
—Jon Kabat-Zinn

Acknowledgments

Thank you, God, for giving me life.

Thanks to my wife, Mireille; my sons, Ralph and Paolo; and my daughter, Cynthia, for bringing joy into my heart and for being patient and supportive.

Thanks to my family members, relatives, colleagues, friends, the persons I've worked for and the persons who've worked for me. And, finally, thanks to all the people who have crossed my path.

Thanks to my family at the Mars Venus coaching organization.

Thanks also to Joe Chalhoub, who inspired me.

Special thanks to Raymonde Habbaki Abou Diwan and my coach, Rich Bernstein, who not only motivated me but also contributed to the editing of this book.

Thank you Father Joseph Tohme for supporting me. Thank you for introducing me to different occasions. Your words and preaching have many times touched me in different ways. God bless you.

I love you all for being part of my life experiences.

I would like to take this opportunity to thank all the writers who have inspired me. They helped me get a wider angle on the world, see life from different perspectives, and state my own vision assertively: Anthony Robbins, Bob Proctor, Christie Marie Sheldon, Daniel Goleman, Deepak Chopra, Eckhart Tolle, Francis Collins, Gibran Khalil Gibran, James Redfield, John Gray, Joyce Meyer, Martin Seligman, Maxwell Maltz, Omraam Mikhael Aivanhov, Rhonda Byrne, Richard Wiseman, Robert McPhillips, Robin Sharma, Ron L. Deal, David H. Olson, and Stephen Covey.

Contents

Foreword

As the president and CEO of Mars Venus Coaching Global, a network of coaches, I recruit and train coaches in twenty-nine different countries around the world. I have seen many different personalities and profiles of the coaches and clients we serve. None see the world the way Marcel does. I realized this the first time I met him. After my meeting with Marcel, I discussed him with our founder, John Gray, author of *Men Are from Mars, Women Are from Venus* and eighteen other books that have become a global phenomenon. John asked me to tell him about Marcel and why he would be a good coach on our team. I thought for a minute, and somehow I couldn't put my finger on it. I said, "Let me think." After careful thought I said, "He's happy. Marcel is at peace."

When Marcel told me he was planning to write this book, I told him I would be honored to write the foreword, as I knew his story would touch lives around the world. His observations of people and where they are in their understanding of the world both internally and in relation to the rest of the world are brilliant. This book will change your perspective on where happiness comes from and how to tap into the energy that happiness can bring you. You will never wonder how to achieve it again, and, more important, once you feel real happiness, you'll be able to maintain it with his techniques. He lets you see his authentic self, from the time when he was not happy and lost everything through a real-life journey on everything he tried all the way to realizing his best life today. It's really an amazing adventure—one that we have all felt to some degree but probably never realized.

I was personally touched by his stories. I found myself relating to every part of this book, and I know the more I read it, again and again, I will see other applications in different aspects of my life. The exercises helped me break down the processes and use them today. Right now. The results are immediate.

I recommend you read this book, as it will change the way you see your thoughts, your feelings, and your relationships. You'll make everyone you know read it as well. Thank you, Marcel, for being part of my life.

I recommend this book with pride.

Richard Bernstein
CEO, Mars Venus Coaching

Writing beyond words.

Reading this book helped me see through Marcel, all the way to the person who was behind it. Authenticity is its key characteristic. And so is what I call "logical emotion." Marcel gives emotions the right to be…for people to see beyond and overcome their own weaknesses. Anger, sadness, and fear are questioned, accepted, and fought back so that joy and happiness take the lead in one's life. Not only will this book's readers learn to identify daily mechanisms and ways for dealing with life, but they will also learn the process of how to go beyond what's stepping in their way and to move ahead with their dreams.

Marcel's book is based on both a synthesis of renowned authors of positive psychology and religion—he gives them due credit and homage—and on his personal thoughts, experiences, and beliefs.

By staying true to himself, Marcel goes beyond the boundaries of clichés and regulations. However, his values and core guidance rules are set as a clear flicker to his flame. His mission and vision will inspire whoever digs into his words' real meanings and true experiences and deconstruct one's typical programmed path in order to build on solid ground. A book for believers or nonbelievers—and one that definitely targets those who believe that there is something more to life, or whatever goes beyond.

Marcel's book was valuable guidance for me in chaotic times. A kind of anchor that made me face my question marks and look inside my inner self to find answers. His words hold empathy and encouragement to move forward in one's quest for answers. Reading his book, it felt as if his words had their own voice—his.

Thank you, Marcel. Time is precious. And you give it so genuinely.

Marie-Christine Tayah
Writer, translator, and editor-in-chief

How I Started

It all began one day when I was watching a TV movie that I don't even remember the name of—but one very important scene changed my whole life.

A teacher asked the twelve-year-old children in her class to read the obituary page of the newspaper as a homework assignment. She then asked them to write their own obituaries by imagining what people would say about them, the day they died, and their achievements.

I was really impressed by this exercise. I asked myself: "What would my children say to *their* children about their grandfather and his achievements?"

I could come up with *no answer* to this question. I was shocked.

I spent fifteen years of my life in Africa. I lost all my various businesses and my investments. I never built anything. I never wrote a book. I never taught anything. I never did any community work. The only answer I could come up with was that I was not a *bad* person (according to my belief system), but the only achievement I had made at the age of fifty was that I had raised a beautiful family of three kids the best way I knew how.

I wanted to achieve something, but what could I do at this age? I didn't even have enough money to leave an inheritance for my children, and I didn't think I had any free time to help in the community. Then a very stupid—but inspiring—idea came to mind. The decision was made.

I called my wife, Mireille, and told her, "When I die, I want everyone to say that I lived every single minute left of my life *happy*."

The commitment was made, but the big question was how to get there. Could anyone be happy all the time?

Is it possible to feel constantly peaceful?

Is it possible not to get angry—ever?

Is it possible not to feel fearful or not to worry?

Is it possible to live without nagging problems?

Is it possible to have all my needs met and to live respectfully of others?

Is it possible to control other people's behaviors and actions toward me?

I invite you to accompany me on the journey I took trying to answer these questions. It turned out that during my struggle for happiness, I discovered an entirely different world that had been there around me the entire time.

One World, Different Views

The world I discovered during my journey to find happiness was actually the same world I had always lived in. Seeing it through a different perspective, with different knowledge, and with a different awareness, however, it looks like another world entirely, and it's much more enjoyable and meaningful. This new outlook has changed the way I live my life, my feelings, and my behaviors.

Here is a summarized comparison of my two worlds according to my experience, knowledge, and feelings. For contrast, I have named the two worlds "Yester-World" and "Today-World."

MY YESTER-WORLD

- Material possessions, accompanied by worries about them
- Stress created by deadlines, time pressures, and financial obligations
- Anxiety about and fear of change
- Negative thoughts—sometimes
- Regrets and guilt
- Longing for security and inner peace
- Selfishness, sarcastic attitude, and jealousy
- Fear of death and wondering about the purpose of life and life after death
- Temperamental, angry, arrogant, judgmental, nonaccepting, indifferent behaviors

- Bad listener
- Constant worry about the future
- Emptiness

MY TODAY-WORLD

- Material possessions, accompanied by a feeling of abundance
- Freedom from time pressures and stress
- Wisdom, adaptability, and satisfaction
- Positive thoughts, problems viewed as opportunities for self-learning and self-improvement
- Inner peace and security
- Acceptance, understanding, empathy, humbleness, no judgments, friendliness, and trust
- Sense of personal immortality—belief that the death of the body is a shifting of the soul from the material world to the spiritual world
- Forgiveness and unconditional love
- Enjoying the present, enjoying nature, and enjoying people
- Fulfillment, power, harmony, joy, and permanent happiness

To *tune in* to my Today-World, I had to acquire certain knowledge, skills, and practice. Don't worry. It is simpler than it sounds! The purpose of this book is to describe the guidelines and the process that led *me* to find *real* happiness.

I have divided the process into four parts:

- The first part is about shifting my understanding of the physical world.
- The second part is about shifting my understanding of the spiritual world.
- The third part is about shifting my understanding of my inner world.
- The fourth part is acquiring "happiness intelligence."

Part 1
My Understanding of the Physical World

Boundaries

Two important realizations about the physical world that I learned during this journey helped me to understand the importance of planning, setting goals, and dreaming. But before I talk about those facts, I would like to talk about boundaries.

Our perceptions are usually set by the *boundaries* of what we believe, what we experience, and what we learn; therefore, we have difficulty accepting anything beyond those parameters.

Let us look at some examples:

- A closed mind will be immune to any evidence of love, while an open mind will look out on that same world and find infinite expressions of love.
- The universe is lightless to a blind cave fish, which has evolved to exclude any visual stimuli.
- The universe has no sound to an amoeba, no taste to a tree, no smell to a dolphin.
- Each creature selects its own range of manifestation according to its range of potential, and the universe respects its boundaries. Just as no literal vision of beauty can affect a blind cave fish and no sweetness of perfume can attract a dolphin any aspect of life that lies outside your own boundaries will not hold any real meaning for you.
- I invite you to free yourself from all boundaries and to open your mind to a new range of potential.

The Energy

Your body and everything you see as material is pure energy. Quantum Mechanics has discovered that atoms and sub-atoms are in fact composed of packets of energy. Take any object and this object disappears from the physical world when examined under an electron microscope. Any physical matter turns into a hazy cloud, and in a step further of magnification, it will vanish into pure invisible vibrations.

—DEEPAK CHOPRA, *AGELESS BODY, TIMELESS MIND*

Leading research on human consciousness is showing that energy vibrates on a Scale of Consciousness.

The Scale of Consciousness was illustrated by Dr. David Hawkins in his book *Power vs. Force*. He showed that consciousness, and therefore each human emotion, has a vibration frequency in the exact same way that matter does.

Heavy emotions like fear, anger, or shame, vibrate at low frequencies and affect your body in negative ways. But feelings like love, joy, and peace vibrate at high, uplifting frequencies.

The scale level goes from the omega—ultimate consciousness—to the lowest point, alpha.

Enlightenment-700-plus
Peace-600
Joy-540
Love-500
Reason-400
Acceptance-350
Willingness-310
Neutrality-250
Courage-200
Pride-175
Anger-150
Desire-125
Fear-100
Grief-75
Apathy-50
Guilt-30
Shame-20

Your body is influenced by the way you think and feel. When you receive bad or good news, this causes a change in your body's energy: the good news makes you feel happy, and the bad news makes you feel sick. When a damaging chemical change occurs, stress and weakness are spread through all your organs.

> *Also your energetic frequency is affected by the energetic frequencies of those around you. When you tell someone good news, he will feel good, and when you tell him bad news he will feel uncomfortable if not bad. And the behaviors of people can steal or increase your energy.*

> —JAMES REDFIELD, *THE CELESTINE PROPHECY*

- Intimidators steal energy from others with threats.
- Interrogators steal energy by judging and questioning.
- Aloof people attract attention (and energy) to themselves by playing coy.
- People who say "poor me" make us feel guilty and responsible for them.
- Happy people increase your energy.

Further, supporting evidence shows that it's not just other people you can affect with your vibrations, but also other objects and even your reality! You are going to see how this works in more detail in the coming chapters.

3

The Power of Thoughts

Your thoughts have a powerful influence. The four statements below are theories that quantum physics and medicine are now beginning to prove, making them startling new realities:

A. YOUR THOUGHTS MENTALLY AFFECT YOUR BRAIN CELLS. THE PROOF OF THIS THEORY IS THE PLACEBO EFFECT.

A placebo (or dummy pill) is an inert substance, typically a tablet, capsule, or other dose of something that does not contain an active drug ingredient. For example, placebo pills or liquids may contain simple starch, sugar, or saline.

Research has shown that a placebo treatment can have a positive therapeutic effect in a patient, even though the pill or treatment is not active. This is known as the "placebo effect" or "placebo response." *The placebo effect is related to the perceptions and expectations of the patient.* If the substance is viewed as helpful, it can actually cause healing, but if it is viewed as harmful by the patient, it can cause negative effects—this is known as the "nocebo effect."

A placebo described as a muscle relaxant will cause actual relaxation, for example, and if described as the opposite, muscle tension.

Similarly, a placebo presented as a stimulant will have the effect of increasing heart rhythm and blood pressure, but when administered as a depressant, the opposite effect will take place.

Because placebos are dependent upon their recipient's perception and expectation, various factors that change the patient's perception can increase the magnitude of the placebo response. For example, studies have found that the color and size of the placebo pill makes a difference. "Hot-colored" pills work better as stimulants, while "cool-colored" pills work better as depressants. Capsules, rather than tablets, seem to be more effective, and size can make a difference. One researcher has found that big pills increase the effect, while another has argued that the effect of size is dependent solely upon cultural background. More pills, branding, past experience, and high price increase the effect of placebo pills. Injections and acupuncture cause even larger effects than pills. A deep-seated belief in the efficacy of a placebo is associated with decreased mortality.

The placebo effect can work selectively under the influence of various psychological factors. If a placebo cream is applied on one hand with the expectation that it is an analgesic, it will reduce pain only on that hand—not elsewhere on the body. If a person is given a placebo under one name and the person responds, he or she will respond in the same way on a later occasion to that placebo under that name, but not if it's administered under another name.

The brain's involvement in the placebo effect has been researched in the following ways:

- Parkinson's disease: Placebo relief is associated with the release of dopamine in the brain.
- Depression: Placebos for reducing depression affect many of the same areas that are activated by antidepressants, with the addition of the prefrontal cortex.
- Caffeine: Placebo-caffeinated coffee causes an increase in bilateral dopamine release in the thalamus.
- Glucose: The expectation of an intravenous injection of glucose increases the release of dopamine in the basal ganglia of men (but not women).

What is a nocebo effect?

A nocebo effect is the opposite of the placebo effect. It is a negative psychological effect from a treatment with no actual pharmacologic value. This can occur when the placebo is administered and accompanied by the suggestion that the patient's ailment might get worse. High nocebo effects can also interfere with the interpretation of clinical-trial results. A drug's negative effects may therefore be due to psychological nocebo effects and not necessarily to the drug itself.

B. YOUR THOUGHTS AFFECT YOUR BLOOD CELLS.

Numerous other studies have shown that a conscious or sentient being, like a human being, can change what happens to another object by affecting that object's energy. Dr. William Braud's research resulted in very compelling evidence that this could happen.

Dr. Braud and his colleagues at the Mind Science Foundation in San Antonio, Texas, designed and conducted some of the most ingenious and rigorous experiments in bio-PK, the study of how psychokinesis affects other biological organisms. They showed that people could slow down the rate at which red blood cells die in a petri dish by mentally willing the blood cells to stay alive. Though the effect was admittedly a small one, the results proved significant beyond chance and were replicable by other scientists.

C. YOUR THOUGHTS AFFECT EVERYTHING AROUND YOU.

Another fascinating and famous research study that shows evidence of people affecting the energy of objects was conducted by Dr. Masaru Emoto. He projected a thought onto a glass of water or put the water next to a specific object. Then the water was frozen and the resulting water crystals were observed under the microscope.

High-energy frequencies, like "love" thoughts, formed crystals in the water in beautiful patterns that were pure in color and in perfect symmetry. Low-energy frequencies, like "anger" thoughts, formed crystals in the water that were rough, dull in color, and in a state of disarray.

D. YOUR THOUGHTS AFFECT YOUR REALITY.

Keep in mind that everything in this universe—whether or not you can see it with the naked eye—is an expression of energy. Also bear in mind that energy operates by exact laws. You are subject to those laws, in just the same manner nature is.

I like how Bob Proctor—in his book *You Were Born Rich*—described what he terms "vibrational interaction":

Visualize an acorn. Then think—really think—about what it is you are looking at. Although the acorn may appear to be a solid object, by now you should clearly understand that the acorn, like everything else which appears to be solid, is in truth, "a mass of molecules at a very high speed of vibration." Within the acorn, there is a nucleus or a patterned plan that dictates the vibratory rate at which these molecules will move. Moreover, the same principle holds true for all seeds. In other words, every seed has a nucleus or a patterned plan within it, which dictates the vibration it will be in and which thereby governs the end product into which it will expand or grow.

However, as soon as you plant the acorn in the earth, the patterned plan or the vibratory rate of the acorn sets up an attractive force and the acorn begins to attract everything that vibrates in harmony with it to expand and grow into an oak tree.

Thoughts alter the vibrational signature of our personal energy field, and send that signal out to the rest of the universe. Every conscious being in the universe is constantly sending out, and receiving from, the rest of the universe. Every particle, every cell, in the universe is conscious, and everything in the universe is responding to everything else, through vibrational interaction.

We may understand that everything in the universe is conscious by simply observing the process of cell division. The material of the cell, and the elements within it, self-organize; the material within the cell re-arranges itself such that a duplicate cell is literally created from the material of the first cell. Merely by observing this process, it becomes evident that the cell itself is programmed to perform certain tasks, which it does efficiently and effectively, over and over again, millions of times every day. This programming is not arbitrary; clearly and indisputably, it is intelligent. The cellular programming is the result of consciousness. The cell is conscious, it is aware, and it knows what it is doing, every time.

What exactly does it mean that a person is broadcasting a "vibrational signal" to the universe?

In our vibrational model, each thought is a vibration, a frequency. Think of each thought as if it were a combination of waves, each of a certain shape, amplitude, and frequency, like a sound wave. Think of it as the type of waveform that a piece of music will make when it is graphed on a computer screen.

(1) A thought can be modeled as a unique combination of waveforms, which has an overall pattern of vibration.

An analogy would be the experiments in vibration conducted by the German researcher Hans Jenny, who used sound, electricity, and other vibrational stimulation to produce clearly defined visual models of vibrational effects.

(2) In the vibrational universe model, so too does thought produce a specific vibrational pattern, depending upon its content.

What should we take away from this scientific evidence of interconnection? If we are persuaded that the subtle structuring of random data does indicate an effect of human attention and emotion in the physical world, it broadens our view of what consciousness means. One implication is that our attention matters in a way we may not have imagined possible and that cooperative intent can have subtle but real consequences. This is cause for reflection about our responsibilities in an increasingly connected world. Our future holds challenges of planetary scope that will demand both scientific clarity and mutual cooperation. On this we should be of one mind.

HOW THEN IS THE INTERACTION OF VIBRATION FROM EVERYTHING IN THE UNIVERSE TO EVERYTHING ELSE IN THE UNIVERSE MANAGED?

Your focus determines the content of your broadcast signal to the universe, and what comes to you in response is an identical match to that signal. The answer is, through the all-powerful universal law known as "like attracts like." The principle is that what is *activated* is what is *broadcasted*.

HOW DOES THIS SO-CALLED LAW OF ATTRACTION WORK?

Place your attention on those things that are wanted, and don't fight against what is not wanted. Fighting, fearing, or worrying about something places your attention on it, so you get more of it in return.

We not only attract what we think about; we also repel its opposite! Focusing your attention on what you do *not* want sends out a kind of force into the universe that repels conditions for what you *do* want. When you feel insecure about your financial future, you are actually repelling your opportunity for greater financial success. When you think of a person who causes you to feel angry, you are repelling the personality types that arouse your feelings of love. When you think of a relationship you find disturbing, you are repelling any relationship that could arouse your feelings of satisfaction. The more you think about the kind of person and the kind of relationship you do *not* want in your life, the more you repel the kind of person and the kind of relationship you *do* want in your life. Out of fear, you are holding onto ideas or visualizations of what scares you the most. The part of you that is holding onto those visualizations is doing so because it believes that to hold onto that experience keeps it away—but it actually attracts it to you.

Fear, anger, disappointment, and hatred send out a force of repulsion. Trust, acceptance, appreciation, and love emit a force of attraction. That is the relationship secret of the law of repulsion, in a nutshell. The experience you hold in your mind takes up "space" in your life.

To use the law or power of repulsion wisely is to focus on the actual power of love that rules our lives and composes the energy of reality. As you allow your heart to fill with this divine and perfect love that is *really* all that exists, you automatically repel people and circumstances that operate in ways that are inconsistent with it.

The only "things" that prevent you from experiencing the perfectly loving relationship that you are having with reality are not things at all— they're the disturbing thoughts and images that darken your mind and trouble your heart.

Negative people find positive people repulsive. As you dwell in love, you will naturally attract more loving people into your life and naturally repel those who might have contrary agendas. Use this relationship secret to attract more of what you want and to repel more of what you don't want.

Ask, Believe, Receive

4

My Background

I was born in one of the smallest and most beautiful countries in the world, Lebanon, in a small city called Jounieh—as beautiful as Monaco and the French Riviera. I lived with my loving parents and sister in a humble, small house. It was cold in winter, hot in summer, but always filled with love.

Being born and raised in a Christian family, I was educated to believe in God and to love Him out of fear of the judgment day. I prayed every night, asking for God's forgiveness. My father had his special way in believing—without hastening to church—while I used to go on Sundays only to satisfy and please my mother. As I grew older and my mother's influential impact on me lessened, I limited my visits to church to sacred holidays: Christmas and Easter.

Why, and what happened?

This was probably due to three reasons. First, I had doubt in some of the beliefs I had been taught, mostly due to the nonmotivating way Christian doctrine was taught to me. Religion classes just seemed like I was studying history. In addition to going to church with my mother on Sundays, we were obliged in school from the years 1960 to 1975 to have one-hour religion lessons and to attend at least one mass a week. Second, religion set boundaries that gave me a feeling of guilt every time I wanted to cross them. Third, most of the priests and nuns in my school and village came from poor families. They had been sent to study and live in the seminary or convent at a very young age, not from any sense of devotion, but only to relieve their families from the burden and expense of raising them. Most of the religious people I encountered came out of the convents and seminaries heartless and rude, angry about life—they showed no mercy. Those nuns and priests were our teachers. How could they succeed at teaching about Christianity's love when they had never experienced it themselves?

My guiding principles for life were limited to the Ten Commandments: live by them and you go to heaven, otherwise you go straight to hell. Living within these boundaries, life looks like one big prison. Most of our religious teachers also do not lead by example—they do not live by what they preach.

When I was eighteen years of age, the war in Lebanon started. We had to live under bomb shellings. No more universities. No more work. No more dreams. I started questioning even more of what had been taught to me about the spiritual world because what I had been taught wasn't providing me any answers to my questions that seemed logical:

Why is life not fair?

Why is God not fair?

Why aren't all people equal?

Why is there a lot of poverty?

Why are people getting killed for no reason?

And the biggest question that tormented me was: Does God really exist?

The loving and caring God I had prayed to and learned about in school, was He the same God who was supposed to be acting on Earth right then?

I think everyone has gone through similar dilemmas; some of you have probably solved them, and some have not.

As a child, I lived with the fear of punishment most of the time—children always break some of the rules, at home and at school. I was not an excellent student and I hated studying, so the worry of failing haunted me, too. Life at school was not always fair and was full of discrimination.

During the war, I came to live in a permanent state of fear, instability, and insecurity. My father became unemployed. Luckily, my mother ran a small sewing school, and the little earned helped us survive. I gave up my dream of becoming a dentist because attending a university was not affordable. Instead, I was more concerned about how to work and study at the same time. I took on many manual labor jobs whenever I heard of something available: on cargo ships, on a plantation, and in an electric plant. With the little money I earned, I attended an evening school and studied accounting. After three years, I graduated.

I started my independent journey as an adult with skills that had nothing to do with my early dreams.

At the age of twenty-one, I wasn't an evil or a destructive person; however, bad habits had become part of my character. I was always angry, envious, jealous, greedy, arrogant, and full of hatred, superiority, and ego. Despite all of that, I considered myself a good person. According to what I had been taught, truly bad people were those who stole, killed, or physically harmed someone.

The meaning of happiness for me then was tied up with possessing new things, flirting around, meeting friends, and exercising my leadership.

5

Prosperous Period

I worked for two years in Beirut; I was promoted very quickly from an accountant to an administrative assistant. I traveled to Lagos, Nigeria, in 1981, and spent fifteen years holding managerial positions and preserving two great habits: optimism and gratitude.

During this period abroad, I was lucky to marry Mireille. She gave birth to our three wonderful children: Cynthia, Ralph, and Paolo. I was well paid and had a high standard of living, combined with a work-life balance.

Real estate was booming in England, so I invested in a partnership by using some of my savings on a down payment for an apartment in London, and I used the other part in Lagos to start up a new company with two partners, dealing with the import and distribution of consumables, food, and beverages.

Success followed swiftly. The company in Lagos built up an image of trust and prosperity. Investors and dealers were attracted to us. French, Italian, English, and Lebanese suppliers offered a very wide range of goods with long-term payment options.

After three years, we decided to expand our business into a new line of activities. In partnership with another company, we purchased a shoe factory—complete with machinery and equipment. The plant capacity was enough to produce one thousand pairs of men's and women's shoes and sneakers per day.

Personally, I bought an apartment almost at cost in a prestigious area in Lebanon, thanks to a very good friend. The building was in the planning phase. No down payment was even requested—only payment by monthly installments.

Money was coming in, business was growing, my family and friend relationships were very good, and entertainment and distractions were available. Life couldn't be better, right? Well, the pleasure of success was always accompanied by a feeling of personal and business insecurity. There were a lot of robbery incidents, roads were not safe in the evenings, and most of the time we had to make a car convoy to cross from one region to another. I had to keep a loaded gun under my bed while I slept even though my apartment was well secured. The political and economic situation was also not good—in Nigeria the situation was never stable, and that gave me a permanent feeling of anxiety.

By the way, I want to share with you what I have learned about anxiety: the body's reaction to anxiety is the same as its reaction in a fight-or-flight situation, just with no specific threat. This feeling is happiness's biggest enemy, and it is the number-one energizer for stress.

6

Down Period

When I bought the London apartment, the plan had been to redecorate it, furnish it, and lease it, hoping that the rental revenue would cover the monthly installment payments. Just as the apartment became ready, however, Iraq invaded Kuwait, banks in Europe froze many Iraqis' and Kuwaitis' accounts, the Arabians lessened the frequency of their visits to the UK, the level of demand for rental properties became low and for a period of one year, our agent in London couldn't lease the apartment—not even for a week. Due to the war, all properties in London lost 30 percent of their values and, at that point, I could not keep paying my monthly installments while the house continued to lose value. What money I did have was needed for the new company I had established. So I decided to cut my losses and release my ownership to my partner, without any returns.

Three years passed, and the company was growing because of the credit facilities lines granted to us by our French and English suppliers. The shoe-making machines were cleared through customs, and the plans for machinery installation and recruiting were under review. Just then, Nigeria's military government was due to organize a democratic election. To understand what happened next, I need to explain the country's background a bit. The country is divided into three ethnic groups: Yoruba, Igbo, and Hausa. The Hausa dominated all the army's highest positions, and Hausa people believe that the presidential position must always be theirs. The election resulted in a surprise: the majority of votes went to a Yoruba candidate. The new candidate claimed his presidential position, but the army decided to put him in jail, claiming there had been fraud in the election process. Guess what happened? Riots started all over the country, there was no more work, the local currency was devalued by 80 percent against the US dollar, and the US dollar lost 20 percent against European currency.

Within six months, my company's business situation looked like this:

- Our goods like milk, cheese, and other short shelf-life products all expired.
- No new sales came in, but our previously ordered products kept arriving.
- Our debtors had no money to pay us, and the money we did collect was worth less than one-fifth of its original value.
- Our foreign creditors still wanted their money.
- We put the shoe-plant machinery on the market, but no one wanted to buy it.
- The company's cash flow was in deficit and we could not pay our creditors' bills.

At the same time, my family left for Lebanon because it was risky—we often had to bring the children from school by boat because roads were closed and unsafe. Over the next three months, without my family around, I began to feel lonely and disappointed in myself. After fifteen years of hard work in Nigeria, I had ended up with no money, no savings. I was unmotivated, had no energy to stay, and would have to start all over and make something work again. I released my equity in the company without any returns and started planning a way to get back to Lebanon.

But before leaving Nigeria, I drew up a preliminary plan to manufacture ham and sausage products in Lebanon, and I offered the plan to a businessman who owned a cold-storage facility in Beirut. He was ready to invest. On my way to Lebanon, I visited France to connect with several factories and suppliers. Once in Beirut, while completing the feasibility study for the project, my future business partner lost a large amount of money: the military government in Nigeria had decided to cancel all log licenses issued the year before and stopped all licensees from shipping what was ready to be exported, and this affected him. I lost the only investor I had for the project.

After fifteen years of work in Nigeria, my financial situation looked like this:

- I had US $2,000 in hand and a family of six.
- Since I had no resources to continue making the installment payments on the new apartment in Lebanon, I had to cancel my apartment's purchase contract.
- Five months before my arrival back in Lebanon, my late father's estate underwent a heritage distribution, and when I arrived, I decided to sell my part. The money I received was enough to get an apartment in an average area and to furnish the forty-square-meter office that I'd bought twelve years earlier to start an accounting office—back to my initial profession. What a failure. I had only one client, and business for him was so bad that he could not pay me.

I was back to square one. No money—sometimes I couldn't even afford bread. I owe a big debt of thanks to my wife's family for their generous support and for providing food, and thanks to friends who loaned me money. This situation lasted about a year, during which I was looking for *any* administrative or accounting job. The experience I had acquired in Nigeria was not relatable to any market other than Africa's, unfortunately. I was ready to accept any salary, but everywhere I went I was told I was either overqualified or underqualified.

After fifteen years of hard work and becoming accustomed to wealth, I found myself at forty responsible for a family of six, without money or work, with only limited skills. I was feeling victimized, neutralized, and unsuccessful.

Never in my life had I thought that I would be in such a situation, but it happened. Usually people react to similar situations by using two different types of self-talk: negative self-talk called *reactive language,* or positive self-talk called *proactive language.* I tried both.

In reactive language, my self-talk went like this: "There is nothing I can do. Fate is against me. I can't fight my destiny. If only I had been more careful with my spending. If, if, if…" I would feel victimized, not in control. I was blaming fate, blaming political issues, and blaming others.

In proactive language, my self-talk went like this: "I will keep looking for something else. I will find a different approach. I choose to fight, and I will come out of this mess." This attitude would make me feel self-confident, in control, able to find a solution, responsible, and optimistic. These feelings would make me happy instead of sad and depressed.

If you were in my shoes, which self-talk language would you use?

How would you feel?

How would you behave?

7

Seeking Help

In the end, I chose to use proactive language.

I checked the daily newspaper announcements for opportunities. I sent my curriculum vitae to all my relations and contacts. I went to several job interviews—without success.

Luckily, this situation did not affect my marriage. My wife never complained, she never made me feel like a failure. She had faith in me, she was happy when I was home, and I don't know how she managed to keep her beautiful smile on her face the whole time. She deserved my respect, love, and admiration. I dedicated my leisure time to my children, and we played and participated in whatever free activities we could find.

I forgot to tell you about the vow I had taken before traveling to Nigeria. When I was a child, my mother sometimes took us to pray and spend the day with other families in a nearby village where an icon of the Virgin Mary was kept in a cave. I kept the positive feelings I gained during those picnics in my memory. So before traveling, I visited the cave, and when praying, I promised the Virgin Mary that if I came back home safely from Africa, I would bring flowers to her every week in homage. I had done this faithfully ever since I had arrived back in Lebanon.

Considering my hopeless situation, I switched to asking for help during my prayers. During my weekly visit, I would pray to God and the Virgin Mary to help me get a job and help me get out of my situation. The weeks passed, and my prayers were not answered.

I began to wonder why we pray when we know, deep down, that most of our prayers will not be answered? Is it because prayers help us keep hoping that whoever created the world can change our situation?

Have you ever asked yourself this question—why so few people have their prayers answered? Have you wondered about the people whose prayers are answered? Are they favored in God's eyes? Do they pray more? Are they better people? Do they love God more? Is it really an act of God at all, or is it a simple act of luck?

In all my relationships and in all my life experiences, I have never once heard someone say his or her prayers had been answered—other than a few stories about health miracles. And in the cases where those prayers were actually answered, the person deep down in his or her heart and mind couldn't be sure if it happened by luck, by coincidence, or actually because of the prayers.

Nevertheless, even though my reasoning side said there was no use to it, I kept going to the cave and praying. I had never read the Bible or any religious book, and the only prayers I knew were the ones I had learned at school. In the cave, they displayed a big, open Bible, and out of sheer curiosity I read the two visible pages one day. What was written on the page simply affected me in the same way as a history book, though, nothing more, and the minute I left, all was forgotten.

One day, the Bible was open to Mark 11:22–25: *Jesus said to them, "Have faith in God. I tell you the truth, if someone says to this mountain, 'Be lifted up and thrown into the sea,' and does not doubt in his heart but believes that what he says will happen, it will be done for him. For this reason I tell you, whatever you pray and ask for, believe that you have received it, and it will be yours. Whenever you stand praying, if you have anything against anyone, forgive him, so that your Father in heaven will also forgive your sins.'"*

I said to myself, "If Jesus is true, then his words must also be true." Being a scientific person, I think in logic and formulas, so I reasoned that if what Jesus said is true, I must be missing something. I figured out that the missing word was "believe." I had never learned how to believe, and deep down I was not sure what to believe in.

I thought it would be easy to make myself believe, but it was not. How could I make my heart follow my mind, even though my mind lacked knowledge? It wanted to believe, but my heart was full of worries and uncertainty. I kept reading the Bible to try and understand more about this simple, magical formula.

What you are about to read next made me more determined than ever to give Jesus's words a try. Matthew 7:7–11 states, *"Ask and it will be given to you; seek and you will find; knock and the door will be opened for you. For everyone who asks receives, and the one who seeks finds, and to the one who knocks, the door will be opened. Is there anyone among you who, if his son asks for bread, will give him a stone? Or if he asks for a fish, will give him a snake? If you then, although you are evil, know how to give good gifts to your children, how much more will your Father in heaven give good gifts to those who ask him!"*

And also, in Matthew 17:20, Jesus told them, *"I tell you the truth, if you have faith the size of a mustard seed, you will say to this mountain, 'Move from here to there,' and it will move; nothing will be impossible for you."*

Like me, you are probably thinking, "if what Jesus said is true, why isn't it working for the billions of Christians who believe in Him and His words?" And if I suppose that these verses about asking, believing, and receiving are true and if they work, how come the priests are not teaching people how to live by them effectively?

Even though my mind could not understand the big conflict between Jesus's promises and the Christians' way of believing that I had experienced, I was determined to keep on praying. Maybe because I did not have a better option. My next visits to the cave to pray took on a different slant. I asked God and the Virgin Mary to help me find a job and solve my financial problems, and my prayers this time were from the heart. Before leaving I said to Mary, "I am confident that you will take care of all my worries. They are in your hands now. Thank you." Please imagine my feelings—a whole year without a job, financial debts growing, and not knowing what to do next. Every door I had knocked on was closed. I was feeling worried, afraid, stressed, and unhappy. All these feelings were haunting my days and nights. The day I said "I know you will take care of my problems" to

Mary and meant it, however, I felt happiness, hope, and peace when I left the cave.

The problem was that these positive feelings lasted for only a day or two, and then the negative feelings took over again, until my next visit. A month passed and nothing happened. My newfound belief started to erode, and when that happened, I read the verses about the prayer and the parable of the persistent widow in Luke 18:1–8: *Then Jesus told them a parable to show them they should always pray and not lose heart. He said, "In a certain city there was a judge who neither feared God nor respected people. There was also a widow in that city that kept coming to him and saying, 'Give me justice against my adversary.' For a while he refused, but later on he said to himself, 'Though I neither fear God nor have regard for people, yet because this widow keeps on bothering me, I will give her justice, or in the end she will wear me out by her unending pleas.' And the Lord said, 'Listen to what the unrighteous judge says! Won't God give justice to his chosen ones, who cry out to him day and night? Will he delay long to help them? I tell you, he will give them justice speedily.'"*

When I read this, I decided to be persistent with my belief. My negative feelings changed into happiness again, and *when I prayed next, it was with the feeling of great expectation* that a job opportunity was on its way. In order for you to understand the way I felt, imagine you've ordered something you really desire—car, camera, mobile phone, dress—and the supplier has told you that it is not in stock and that it will be ordered for you, but it will take a while. I am sure that knowing this makes you feel that you already own it, and you dream of how to use it or what you'll do with it when it arrives. My expectation gave me the same kind of giddy feelings.

This was my first true spiritual experience. Would it work? Would that help end the twelve-month crisis? And if it happened, would it be attributable to faith, or to pure luck?

8

Help Becomes Available

It seemed that the down period had reached an end.

In November 1996, after sixteen months without employment, I received my first job opportunity thanks to my brother-in-law, a showroom manager for a company that dealt with electronic devices: computers, mobile phones, cameras, music players, and so on. And it happened that I had a love for all these kinds of products, so I was very happy with the job and motivated to do it well, but the salary was not enough to meet my financial obligations.

Six months later, and thanks to my other brother-in-law, I received a position as a senior accountant for a construction company—for double the salary. I stayed there for two years. It was challenging and great, until the project fell into financial difficulties. Due to the high level of stress within the management that ensued, their way of communicating with the employees became unbearable. I decided to resign. Do you think that taking such an action without a backup should be considered reckless? Should I have looked for a new job before resigning? Perhaps, but I had to decide between staying in the job and anticipating a heart attack or leaving the job and facing the financial consequences. Let me remind you that during all this time, my weekly prayers to Mary and my visits to the cave did not stop. My belief that God would not let me down had become part of my life.

And help arrived. Before the end of the two months' notification period I had given the company about my intent to leave, thanks to my third brother-in-law, I received a new opportunity as a senior accountant and office manager for a newly established retail company. I started working with them in July of 1999. I helped the company get established at the administrative level by setting up internal and accounting regulations, stock control, human resource management, and the opening of two new retail branches. Two years passed, and operations were moving along smoothly. I gained a lot of experience in information technology systems, and to improve my accounting skills I took a management accounting course (CMA) after work. I knew that my income would not change as long as I stayed in that company, though, since there was no chance for promotion. I was already occupying the highest position available and I was ready to move on to a different level. Since everything was organized and regulated, and to keep my earnings flowing, I convinced management that my working just two days a week as a financial controller would result in the operation running just as efficiently. I joined as a consultant in management information systems a young auditing firm for the other three days per week, with no fixed salary. I also took a course on ISO quality-management systems. But the flow of customers did not meet my expectations, even though we'd created a website, printed customer brochures, and advertised.

My daughter finished school and was ready to attend a university. My income was not enough to afford to pay her tuition, but I wasn't worried. I knew that God would provide what was needed—somehow. Then I received an offer from a company to work two days a week as a financial controller. This arrangement would still allow me to work one day in another capacity as well for a third association.

Two years later, it was my eldest son's turn to attend a university. The week he registered, I received an offer from the newest association to handle the accounting for three new organizations. I was now living well, and all that I have said so far was also happening before that day that I decided to live every moment happy.

In this introduction to who I am I have included a lot of details that I could have skipped, but I wrote them to point out that you can't know or predict what will happen to your financial situation. You can't control all its elements—there will always be political instability, fluctuations in economic development, and volatile market behavior. I suggest you read the book *The Black Swan* by Nassim Nicholas Taleb for more on this!

We can't face the world's problems and the unforeseeable circumstances all by ourselves. God, who has created us, is waiting to give us help, but we have to start helping ourselves *first*. Do not expect a salary increase or more money if you keep doing the same thing in the same way.

If you keep doing the same thing in the same way, you will keep getting the same result.

To live a great life, you have to open your boundaries to a new level of awareness—this will help you get all the help you want.

9

Experiencing the "Ask, Believe, Receive" Theory

In 2006, I was listening to a TV program discussing the content of the book *The Secret* by Rhonda Byrne. As I listened, I noticed that I had experienced most of what the book was saying. I decided to read the book for myself, and I found that what I was living was similar to what many people on a similar path had experienced. But, there were two themes it discussed that I had not yet considered or tried:

- The world is full of abundance, and you don't have to feel guilty if you ask for more of it.
- Try exercising "ask, believe, receive" in every area of life.

I suggest that you read *The Secret*. In fact, though, this secret is not a secret! It was revealed by Jesus Christ as mentioned in my previous chapter and has been used by many Christians. The way it is described in the book gives you more insight, but here is how my life looked when I applied ask, believe, receive:

ASK, BELIEVE, RECEIVE FOR MY HEALTH

As I said in the introductory chapter, my prayers for money were always answered. When I finished reading the *The Secret*, it just so happened that I had a pain in my right hand, and an X-ray showed that the pain was due to multiple calcifications in my right shoulder. The doctor asked for an MRI, and planned surgery. I was also having a problem with my eyes. Being on the computer for more than twelve hours a day had caused me pain, and I became obliged to use two sets of eyeglasses—one for near vision and the other for far vision. This was very disturbing for me. I decided not to use the eyeglasses anymore, and not to undergo the operation; I started to pray to Mary ten times a day and to recite the "Our Father" prayer ten times a day. After each prayer I said the following:

Thank you, God, for healing my shoulder. Thank you, God, for healing my eyes.

You may ask why I thanked God before it happened. Advance thanking simply helps your heart believe what your mind is asking for and sets you in a mode of expectation.

Two weeks later, the pain in my hand vanished. I got new X-rays on my shoulder and asked the hospital to compare the old and new X-rays. The result was amazing. Instead of multiple calcifications, there was no calcification at all. As for my eyes, after two months of pain and persistence and not wearing eyeglasses, my sight recovered, and I had no further pain. I was again able to read even the tiniest print written on my medicine bottles. It was so strange; I checked my eyes at an optician, and there was no change in my prescription per se, but the simple fact is that I have not used eyeglasses ever since.

ASK, BELIEVE, RECEIVE FOR MY SON'S HEALTH

My oldest son, Ralph, fell at age sixteen and tore the cross ligaments in his knee. At the hospital, the doctor recommended we wait until he was eighteen to do surgery.

Two years later, a friend of his had the same type of accident and did surgery immediately. Meanwhile, my son didn't feel any pain, and from time to time, he was even able to play basketball normally. So we decided to ask his friend's doctor about the consequences if he never had the operation; he said that my son might eventually have arthritis in his knee.

Based on that, we went to a well-known specialist and got a new MRI. The doctor advised us to undergo the surgery. We rushed to try to have the surgery during the university's Easter holidays, but because there was only a little time left on his vacation they couldn't fit him in and we postponed it until September. Once it was postponed, I began praying twenty times every day: "Thank you, God, for healing my son's knee." In July, as I was visiting with my son at the cave to pray, I told him, "Why don't you pray as I do, by thanking God in advance for curing your knee?"

"How can I be convinced that God will do that when I see a lot of people praying who do not get their needs met?" he asked.

We left the location, and I had the feeling that my son was going through a lot of uncertainty with his faith. It was the same feeling I had when I was his age—although unlike me, he goes to church often on Sundays and he does a lot of community work.

As we were getting ready for the surgery, we called the health insurance company for the necessary preauthorizations, and the company responded that they had stopped dealing with our selected doctor. We would have to consult another.

My wife's nephew, who is a doctor and whom I love like a son, referred us to one of his colleagues. During the couple of days before the appointment date, I asked God to give us a sign that my son's knee had healed on its own. I had been praying for him for four months and I requested, as a sign, that my son would suddenly feel a strong pain in the knee—to make the doctor ask for new tests. A week passed with no sign of pain, and I was confused about what to believe. As I was praying on Friday before the next Monday's appointment, I began thinking, "Who am I to tell God what to do and how to do it? All I have to do is believe, and God will do the rest." When I reached home, I told my family and friends that I was sure there would be no surgery necessary.

We went to see the doctor on Monday as scheduled. During the fifteen minutes we were waiting to meet with him, my son and I had the following discussion:

He asked, "Dad, you keep on saying that we will not need do the surgery—based on what logic have you made that assumption? All odds are against us, and *God* did not give you the sign that you asked for."

I replied, "*God's* acts cannot always be explained by logic; if they could be, they would not be called miracles."

After a close physical examination and reviewing the MRI results, which indicated clearly that the cross ligaments were damaged, the doctor said, "Why do you want to do the surgery? Your son does not feel any pain or any weakness in his knee."

I said, "It is based on another doctor's recommendations, and to avoid arthritis."

He said, "Didn't they tell you that even after the surgery the knee may have arthritis?"

I said, "No."

The doctor replied, "In your son's case, I will not do the surgery. His knee's muscles are very strong and holding the knee as they should. I, for the time being, recommend that if he later feels any weakness in his knee, we reconsider."

As we were leaving the doctor, joy overtook every inch of me. I started to cry. That day, I knew that this miracle was going to help me help my family believe too.

Normally, when someone wants to have a surgery, he or she gets at least two doctors' opinions—what happened could be a coincidence. Perhaps, but to me this coincidence was the answer to my prayers.

ASK, BELIEVE, RECEIVE FOR THE COMMUNITY

During my search for happiness, I found out that the most rewarding feeling comes from giving a gift to someone. The giver's happiness is much more intense than the receiver's. I am sure you have felt the same way after buying a gift for someone you care for or love. I started by helping two friends find jobs in companies I was working for, but this alone was not enough for me. I wanted to do more. So I decided to pray on a daily basis to achieve this goal. Every day while praying, I started saying, "Thank you, God, for giving me the opportunity to help others." I was seeing this goal attained after ten years. I didn't have the money or the time to go and do community work, and this is how helping others looked like to me.

One night, as I was having dinner with friends, I sat down next to a very dear person who was the husband of a colleague. I told him about my faith, my prayers, how God was responding to them, and how I was thinking about writing a book. I would call it *Heaven on Earth*. The next day, I received from him this e-mail:

Dear Marcel,

As a matter of fact, I was so depressed for three days before I saw you. I felt like God sent you to tell me your story, although I keep reading on positive thinking, and I strongly believe that whatever shall be asked in prayers shall be given. Sometimes you feel everything is happening the wrong way. That's what I was feeling a few days before I met you by coincidence.

When you moved next to me in the restaurant and you started telling me your story about what happened with you, I felt I was traveling to another world. From one side I was hearing you, and from the other side, I felt that God sent you to tell me what was happening with you and the joy and happiness you're living in. For the first time in my life, I was losing hope, and I'm known as the optimistic and fighter person who never surrenders. You came just in time, as if the Holy God brought you to tell me, "Watch out—you're losing your faith and taking the wrong way."

I was happy deep inside and astonished because I used to read such stories in books or on TV, and it was the first time that I heard it live from someone I know, and at the right time. This was unbelievable. You'll be astonished to know that I'm working on myself, and a few things happened to me because of my faith (that started to grow) and positive thinking.

I wish a good, happy, and joyful life to you and your family, and I hope to reach that point myself soon.

People need to hear such things, and I'm sure whenever they hear it, they'll change.

Good luck with your book. See you soon. Take care.

During the same week, I called my bank and asked for a line of credit for a real estate project that I will talk about later. The bank referred me to the credit manager, and when I called her, I could tell from her voice that she was down. When I met her later in the week, I asked why she was not happy. It emerged that she had tried to commit suicide on two occasions. I had the same talk with her about life, our generous Creator, and our power to change the way we see things. In the next meeting with her, she surprised me by saying, "Marcel, I don't believe what's happening to me. I said to my husband this morning that I wanted to live and I wanted to be happy again."

The next week, I met with another friend who had an audit firm, and the same thing happened. He had a lot of worries at work, and things were not moving forward. He gained confidence again after our talk and received a new project the same week.

These three beautiful incidents made me aware that God had answered my prayer. He was giving me the opportunity to help others in a way that I couldn't have imagined before. In no time, within twenty days, God gave me the message that my contribution in the community didn't have to be monetary or through community work. And I did not need to wait ten years. It could start immediately, by spreading happiness and faith to others.

The decision was made. I wanted to start giving free seminars to others and planting the seeds of faith and happiness in everyone around me. I gave my first seminar on December 3, 2008.

The only question was, how could I continue to do this, as I was working days and nights? Another decision I made, which surprised my friends and family, was to quit the job that was the most rewarding financially. Instead of dedicating evenings and weekend time to this job, I would devote it to my new dream. I was not worried about how I would cope financially. My only aim was to go for it. To my surprise, the same month that I resigned, I received bonuses and a fee increase from my other clients—covering the same amount I gave up.

I tell you: do not worry. God has different ways to help.

ASK, BELIEVE, RECEIVE FOR EXERCISING VALUES

One day, my managing director made it known that he was not happy with the way the junior accountant we had employed was behaving, and since he was still under the three-month probation period, I was asked to let him go. I knew this person had many financial obligations, and putting him out of work without notice to look for another job would be like killing him. Could I be expected to act without mercy in this case when I was helping friends get jobs elsewhere? What do you think I should have done? Present my own resignation, or ask this person to resign? I decided not to take any immediate action since the probation period would be up in ten days anyway. Instead, I used this time to pray, "Thank you, God, for not making me do what is against my values and my will. Thank you for taking care of this issue." Four days before the end date of the probation period, the junior accountant called me to ask if we were going to keep him on. From the tone of his voice, I suspected that he had been offered another job.

I asked him, "Do you have another offer?"

He said, "Yes."

I said, "Take it."

I can't describe to you how I felt; I nearly cried.

Six months later, we had a new junior accountant working, and she did not get along with the manager either. Again he asked me to be the one to do the firing. I got the same value-contradiction thoughts and, again, did not take immediate action. I started praying again, "Thank you, God, for not making me do what is against my values and my will. Thank you for taking care of this issue."

My next meeting with the manager took place a week later, and he asked me, "Marcel, why haven't you executed my request yet, and what are you waiting for?"

I said, "I will do it now," and moved to sit next to the junior accountant to let her know the management's decision.

Before I said a word, she said to me, "Marcel, I want to tell you something that will not make you happy. I have found a position in another company, and I want to submit my resignation to you today."

She thought that she would make me unhappy because she knew how much I cared for her. I did a good job of faking sadness, but my heart was jumping with joy.

Every time I'm obliged to do or say something that is not aligned with love, honesty, and integrity, I refuse—even if the cost is to resign from a position. The managers were upset over my behavior, but on the other hand, they began to value my personality more and more.

I will talk about personal foundations later, in another chapter, but I want to assure you that when you set a foundation of values for yourself, they will help you choose what is right, and you will not be afraid of the consequences. God will be there to support you. Your conscience, when awake, knows the right thing to do.

ASK, BELIEVE, RECEIVE FOR HELPING PEOPLE

I have a family member, GB, who had been working as a manager in a nightclub restaurant for two years. The business was flagging, so the management decided to change its service concept and recruited a new person to do that. My friend was due to leave at the end of the month, a Friday. He was like a brother to me, and I found myself feeling helpless. I started praying for him: "Thank you, God, for GB's new job." I prayed for fifteen days, ten times a day. Saturday was his first Saturday off in four years, and for this occasion I invited him and his wife to dinner. I was supposed to choose a restaurant. I tried to make a reservation at my favorite place, but did not succeed. I was too busy to find another location. I called GB and told him to choose the restaurant and make the reservation. He called a musician who used to play music and sing at the restaurant where he had been working, and it happened that he was playing that night in a newly opened nightclub restaurant. He booked reservations for us there. While we were dining, the musician arrived and he introduced GB to the owner of the restaurant. After just half an hour of discussion, the manager offered my friend a job! He accepted. At that moment, I was so astonished that I didn't know how to praise and thank God enough. The feeling was more than I could handle, and I started to cry.

This instance made me include many people in my daily prayers—my type of volunteer work. Some of the prayers were answered, and some were not, but I will talk more about that later.

I had a small amount in my savings account for something I was planning to do, when a friend told me he had to go into the hospital for a surgical operation. I knew he needed more money to be able to afford the operation. The amount he needed was around 30 percent of my savings. To be frank, for the first time, the feeling of greed was fighting heavily with my will to help, and the struggle was painful for me because it lasted about four days. In the end, the will to help took over, and I did what was right. That made me very happy—and otherwise I think I would have regretted it for the rest of my life! You will not believe what happened next. A week later, my wife received a gift in cash from her brother. The amount was more than what we had given our friend for his surgery.

After this experience, money ceased to matter that much to me, and my financial contributions to others were, and still are, active. God's blessings overwhelm me in every way.

Here is another short story that reveals how well this approach works. My daughter used to sometimes help a single mother in need who had four young children. One day, after visiting this family, my daughter told us that their washing machine wasn't working and the lady could not cope with the load of laundry she had to do. Like every other person hearing such a story, I felt the urge to help. That particular month, however, I was not able to spare the money needed to buy them a washing machine. My desire to help was enormous, and it kept me thinking the whole weekend. The following Monday, on my way to work, a billboard advertisement displayed a washing machine with a discount of 50 percent. So you don't have to guess what I did: I bought them the washing machine.

What bliss! I have experienced many similar cases. These stories prove to me one of the heavenly laws: when you decide to give to others, all the angels in heaven will help you, too.

ASK, BELIEVE, RECEIVE FOR SIGNS: THE REAL-ESTATE BUSINESS

E-commerce has become so common that even I started working on an e-commerce project—real estate sales and leasing through the web. I did the necessary research and prepared a business plan. The project was meant to be financed under a special long-term financing program with zero interest, and was offered by the central bank through a commercial bank. To guarantee this project, I would need to use my house as collateral. The commercial bank's first round of approval was granted, and the file was sent to the central bank for final approval and financing. My prayer was, "Thank you, God, for giving me this project if it is good for me." (In a later chapter, I will be talking about the difference between the law of attraction and God's protection.) The commercial-bank branch manager had, two years earlier, become a friend and agreed to follow my file as it worked its way through the credit department. Usually, the approval takes sixty days at most. Two months passed, and there was no word. My bank did not get a specific reason from the central bank for this delay. My friend at the bank was sorry for the unexpected delay of the approval, and my answer was, "Do not worry. If it is for my own good, it will happen." That was in December 2010. Meanwhile, the real estate business in the Arab countries was crashing, especially in Dubai. In January, they informed me that the central bank had stopped financing e-commerce ventures for 2011. My friend, the branch manager, called and was sorry when she announced the bad news. I commented, "I am glad it did not get approved because 80 percent of the money was intended for advertising, and since the real estate market is crashing, all my investment in the advertisements would have been lost, and the project as a start-up would not have succeeded. I would have lost the money and been in debt." I felt joyful and grateful to God for his intervention.

ASK, BELIEVE, RECEIVE FOR SIGNS: NOT BUYING A NEW CAR

The salesman offered a promotion on the car we were looking at—a 30 percent discount, and without any down payment.

My wife and I liked this car. It was a small and economical one, and at home we needed one since my two children attended different universities.

My daughter had received a discount on her university tuition as financial aid, in exchange for working in the library. In addition we'd applied for student loans in order to have half of the tuition deferred until after her graduation. Having done that, we thought we could afford the monthly installment for a car in case we decided to buy one.

After I prepared all the documents needed to buy the car on credit, I made my way to turn them in to the salesman. As usual, I visited the cave to pray to Mary and ask her to help me cancel the deal if the purchase of the car would cause me any trouble. I released the documents to the dealer. Normally, the approval process takes two days.

The same day, when I got to the office, I received a call from my daughter and my son simultaneously telling me to stop the deal—their friends were having a lot of technical problems with the same model of car. On the same day, the secretary in the office where I was working advised me not to buy it for the same reason. So I called the car dealer and canceled the deal, taking it as a sign not to buy this car. Or any other car, for that matter.

Two weeks later, my daughter's university advised us that her loan was rejected and the financial aid was canceled due to new regulations. Thank you, God, for your messages. It would have been very difficult for me financially if I'd committed myself to any car purchase.

ASK, BELIEVE, RECEIVE FOR PROSPERITY: BUYING A NEW CAR
I eventually started looking to purchase a new car for my wife again, and there was only one particular car she liked that fit our monthly budget. The deal was that we were to give them our used car as a down payment, and the balance would be paid by monthly installments.

As the particular model we wanted was in high demand, no cars were left in stock, and the next delivery date was in three months. Because of that, the company needed a deposit to hold the car—either cash or our used car. Neither would be possible for us.

When I was in a meeting with my bank manager, a lady I respected, I told her this story. It happened that one of her customers was a car salesman. She phoned him and ordered the car—because of the personal connection, I didn't have to leave any deposit, and after three months, I received the car.

ASK, BELIEVE, RECEIVE FOR PROSPERITY:
BUYING A NEW CAR FOR MY SON

Two months before my son's birthday, I started investigating buying him a car. He was still studying at the university, and, just like every young man, his dream car was a sports car that I couldn't afford. He wouldn't mind a used car, I knew, but it had to be a sports car. Buying one would involve many financial obligations for me in addition to the monthly payments, including unpredictable repairs and the excessive consumption of fuel sports cars' powerful engines require. My monthly budget wouldn't allow me to afford all that, and my desire was complex: because the car had to be new, a sports car, had to have a low price tag, and low fuel consumption.

So I started a new daily prayer: "Thank you, God, for helping me find a car for my son's birthday." A week later, during our usual morning chat while I drove him to the university, he mentioned that he loved the sports car his friend had bought. When I reached the office, I called the dealer, and the salesman said the dealership had exactly the type of car I wanted, with all the qualities I mentioned earlier. The next day, my son took the car on a test drive, and he loved it. He got the car twenty days before his birthday.

ASK, BELIEVE, RECEIVE FOR PROSPERITY:
BUSINESS RESPONSIBILITIES

At six o'clock one evening, while I was working in a client's office, I was called in to a meeting with the CEO and his financial backer. I was informed that one of the programs that we were executing had been badly handled by the project manager (whom we had already dismissed). We had to choose between losing the contract, which would jeopardize our reputation, or finding a way to remedy the situation. Since I had built a reputation for trustworthiness and performance with the financial backer during the previous two years, the CEO asked me during the meeting, "Marcel, can we promise them that we can handle it?" By asking me this question in front of the person concerned, the CEO was forcing me to approve. I was the financial comptroller and had nothing to do with the running of the project—the CEO was of course aware of that. He was just using me to give confidence to our financial backer. I thought that this story would end there, and that we could sort something out.

After they left, the CEO put the entire responsibility on me for making an assessment of the situation and providing a solution to the financial backer—within fifteen days. The time allotted would not be enough to handle this issue, because there was now no project manager. At around eight o'clock that evening, while I was rushing to attend a friend's farewell party, I was trying to think of a solution, and reviewing all the people I knew who could possibly fit into a project-management role, and in a short period of time. I had no one in mind, and then I remembered what I always did in such a case: Why worry when I could ask God for help? So I did. When I reached the farewell dinner, I sat next to the husband of one of my colleagues at work, and then I remembered that he might fit that very profile.

I gave him a summary of the tasks. He was interested, and he had the time to take it on. The next day, I sent his curriculum vitae with my recommendations to the CEO. He was asked to come and meet with the team and to assist in the operation. He took the assignment, met with the financial backer, and proposed a plan to save the project.

I often encountered many similar situations in the various companies that I was working with, and every time the solution was above what I felt I could handle, I asked God for help: "God, I did everything I can possibly think of. It is time to ask you for help. Thank you for helping."

ASK, BELIEVE, RECEIVE FOR PROSPERITY: MONETARY NEEDS

During the period when I had two children enrolled in the university, even though I was working intensely, but due to unpredicted house expenses and other social obligations, I came up $7500 short on my daughter's second tuition installment. The due date was in a week's time, and I was not able to find any way to get such an amount together. The good thing about being in a relationship with God is that you don't worry. So I wasn't worried. It was Friday, and the tuition was supposed to be paid on Monday. After my weekly prayer to the Virgin Mary in the cave, on my way to work, I started asking myself how God would make that money available, and from where. An hour later it occurred to me to request the money from one of my clients as a bonus. Even though he was paying me very well, the good work I had been doing did deserve an extra reward. I went to visit him in the late afternoon and told him matter-of-factly that I needed a bonus of $7,500. The request shocked him.

He said, "First, bonuses are granted, not asked for. Second, how did you come up with that amount?"

I said, "The work I have been doing for the past thirteen months deserves a bonus, and the amount is what I need to pay my daughter's tuition, which is due in two days."

I am sure he was not happy about receiving this request in such a way, but since he respected me and appreciated my work, he gave me the money as a loan to be deducted from my future paychecks. He said he would decide later about the bonus. In the end, I only ever paid back 10 percent of that loan; the balance was granted to me as a bonus, and he soon increased my monthly pay by 50 percent as well.

GOD WILL PROVIDE

My daily life and my family's daily lives became full of similar stories as soon as I decided to give my worries over to God. I have chosen to write some of them here to show you that God wants to put His hand in your hand to make your life easier, joyful, and bearable. I have found peace. Why would I ever be afraid again, when I know that the great power that has created all is carrying me, protecting me, and helping all the people related to me?

Before moving into the next chapter, I want to tell you three stories that I have read (I don't recall the references, and I apologize for that). These stories are examples used to illustrate the different ways God intervenes in our lives.

THE MAN WITH THE HUT AT THE BEACH

A man had an accident with his boat while on a fishing trip, and he found himself alone on one of those small islands in the middle of nowhere. The sun was hot, so he decided to build a shelter from a dry tree's branches and leaves. When he finished, he went for a swim, and on the way back, saw the hut burning. The first thing he did was talk to God (I leave it to you to imagine his angry words), and he said, "Why are you doing this to me? Was it not enough that I ended up alone on the island?" He kept shouting and blaspheming until he passed out from sheer exhaustion.

A human voice woke him, and when he asked the person how he had found him, the person said, "We saw a fire on this island, and since we know that no one lives here, it must have been a sign that there was someone who needed help."

The moral of the story is: do not worry when you are presented with what seems like a difficulty. God has special ways of helping you.

THE WOMAN WHO LOST HER JOB

A single woman with three kids lost her job—her only source of income. She decided to invite her family, friends, and neighbors over for dinner. When the invitees came and saw that many people had been invited, they started asking about the reason behind the gathering. Before she called them to eat she said, "I know that many are wondering if we are celebrating something tonight. Yes, we are. I lost my job two weeks ago, and today we are celebrating my expected new job, because I am sure that God is preparing a better one for me."

The moral of the story is: if you have faith in God, you will know that every time one door closes, it means you should look in a different direction, toward another door. How can you possibly improve any situation if you just keep doing the same thing?

THE SWIMMING MAN

A man who was the only survivor of a boat crash found himself on a deserted island, but he could see another mass of land across the water. He was a man of faith and believed that if he swam, God would help him reach it. After he swam just a few meters, a fishing boat came to help him, but he refused to climb aboard, saying he believed in God, and that he knew God would help him reach the shore. After a few hundred meters he started to weaken, and another boat passed by and offered him help, but he said the same thing. He wanted to rely on God alone to help him swim to the other side. In the end, he drowned and died. When he reached heaven, he asked God, "Why did you allow me to drown? You know I have faith in you."

God replied, "I sent you help two times, and you refused it."

The moral of the story is: many times, before making any new decision, we ask God for help and guidance. He will send us signs through other people, a book, a movie—somehow. But most of the time, our desires are so big that we block all the signs sent to us.

A common example of this is before getting married. We may pray, "Dear, God, if this man or women is not the right person for me, do not allow this union to take place." While you were dating, a friend may have said, "Be careful—your soul mate is cheating on you," or "He is greedy," or "He has a bad temper," or "He's a big liar." Hearing these kinds of remarks, we start giving a lot of excuses for why someone might have said them, or denying them outright. Perhaps we should be more careful and look deeper early on in a relationship to find out if it is really true. The remarks of family members or friends are usually signs meant to enlighten us in a certain situation, but most of the time we don't take them into consideration because they are not what we want to hear, especially not when we believe we're in love.

10

Summary of the Physical World

In Part 1 of this book, we have seen that there are three great truths to acknowledge:

1. Your thoughts are very powerful.
2. The way you think affects your way of life.
3. Ask. If you believe, you will receive.

Remember:

1. Your thoughts affect your mind, your body, your behaviors, and everyone around you. This will be discussed further in Part 3, "My Understanding of the Inner World."
2. The intensity of the image you plant as a seed is affected by how strongly your desire is associated with that image. So the image you desire, your heart, and your mind must all be in harmony. This harmony creates an attractive force that governs your results in life.
3. All physical reality is made up of vibrations of energy—so are your thoughts. Only humans have the ability to change the frequency of their own vibrations. If you're sad and you keep focusing on sadness, you will attract more of it. If you are happy and keep focusing on that, you will attract more happiness. Everything you could ever want is already here; it's up to you to get into harmony with the world around you.

Those who are unaware of this law plant plenty of contradictory images in their minds; they are continually switching vibrations, and that never leads to new progress.

At the same time, many people *are* successfully using the power of thoughts and harnessing the laws of attraction. They ask, believe, receive, and they are getting what they want, but the big question when you start using these powers is this: how will you know that the things you want to be manifested in your life are the right things for *you*?

Let me give you some examples:

How will you know whether what you can afford today, such as a mortgage payment on a house, you will still be able to afford tomorrow, or next year?

How will you know that what you are investing in today will be successful tomorrow?

How will you know that your employment is secure and that if you leave it you can find a better job?

How will you know that the woman or the man that you've been after is the right one for you?

How can you be certain that whatever happens to you is for your own good?

Using these laws will help you get the house, the car, the relationship, and everything else you want, but if you want to be *sure* that what you're getting is for your own good, you need to go to the next level of awareness, which is explained in Part 2 of this book.

Take each of my experiences in the previous chapter—try to find a logical or scientific explanation for how things turned out. You cannot. What happened is not within the natural laws that science or logic can define, so many people will call them miracles. Let me tell you the truth: I made the decision to write this book because my daily life has become a series of small miracles. It is like God wants me to share with Him all my doings, my thoughts, and my feelings. It seems that He doesn't mind if they are small things, like wanting chocolate or getting help with a difficult report or expecting happiness all day, and they have begun to happen so regularly that I can't call them miracles anymore. To me, these manifestations fall under the spiritual natural law dictated in Matthew 6:25–34:

> *Therefore I tell you, do not worry about your life, what you will eat or drink, or about your body, what you will wear. Isn't there more to life than food and more to the body than clothing? Look at the birds in the sky: they do not sow, or reap, or gather into barns, yet your heavenly father feeds them. Aren't you more valuable than they are? And which of you by worrying can add even one hour to his life? Why do you worry about clothing? Think about how the flowers of the field grow; they do not work or spin. Yet I tell you that not even Solomon in all his glory was clothed like one of these! And if this is how God clothes the wild grass, which is here today and tomorrow is tossed into the fire to heat the oven, won't he clothe you even more, you people of little faith? So then don't worry, saying, "What will we eat?" or "What will we drink?" or "What will we wear?" for the unconverted pursue these things, and your heavenly Father knows that you need them. But above all pursue his kingdom and righteousness, and all these things will be given to you as well. So then do not worry about tomorrow, for tomorrow will worry about itself. Today has enough trouble of its own.*

Part 2
My Understanding of
the Spiritual World

11

Father-Child Relationship

When I started giving seminars about my experience with happiness and how God answered my prayers, my philosophy was rejected by many Christians and priests, for three reasons:

Reason One: Ask, believe, receive may create a deception that people will always receive what they ask for, and people will lose faith. They would ask me, "How can ask, believe, receive work with the disabled, the poor, and the sick? What can you tell them if they ask and do not receive?"

In Matthew 11:28–30, Jesus said, *"Come to me, all you who are weary and burdened, and I will give you rest. Take my yoke upon you and learn from me, for I am gentle and humble in heart, and you will find rest for your souls. For my yoke is easy and my burden is light."*

There are facts in life that can't be changed, but we can change the way we look at those facts. We can change the way we feel about them, and we can reduce our pain. And all that is possible with God's help. We only need to ask with faith.

As Saint Paul said in Romans 8:28: *"And we know that in all things God works for the good of those who love him, who have been called according to his purpose."*

In Francis Collins's book *The Language of God*, a scientist presents evidence for belief, and this is what he says:

Consider this: if the most important decision we are to make on earth is a decision about belief, and if the most important relationship we are to develop on this earth is a relationship with God, and if our existence as spiritual creatures is not limited to what we can know and observe during our earthly time, then human sufferings take on a wholly new context. We may never fully understand the reasons for these painful experiences, but we can begin to accept the idea that there may be such reasons. In my case, I can see, albeit dimly, that my daughter's rape was a challenge for me to try to learn the real meaning of forgiveness in a terribly wrenching circumstance. In complete honesty, I am still working on that. Perhaps this was also an opportunity for me to recognize that I could not truly protect my daughters from all pain and suffering. I had to learn to entrust them to God's loving care, knowing that this provided not an immunization from evil, but a reassurance that their suffering would not be in vain. Indeed, my daughter would say that this experience provided her with the opportunity and motivation to counsel and comfort others who have gone through the same kind of assault.

He also says the following:

This notion that God can work through adversity is not an easy concept, and can find firm anchor only in a worldview that embraces a spiritual perspective. The principle of growth through suffering is, in fact, nearly universal in the world's great faiths.

Who is Francis Collins? One of the leading geneticists in the United States and a longtime leader of the human genome project. He grew up agnostic and then became a committed atheist while getting his PhD in chemistry. It wasn't until he attended medical school and witnessed the true power of religious faith among his patients that his worldview began to change. He says:

In this modern era of cosmology evolution and the human genome, is there still the possibility of a richly satisfying harmony between the scientific and spiritual world views? The answer is a resounding yes! In my view, there is no conflict in being a rigorous scientist and a person who believes in God, who takes a personal interest in each one of us. Science's domain is to explore nature. God's domain is in the spiritual world, a realm not possible to explore with the tools and the language of science. It must be examined with the heart, the mind, and the soul—and the mind must find a way to embrace both realms.

In his book, he strongly agrees with what President Clinton said in a speech about the latest completed mapping of the human genome, *"Without a doubt, this is the most important, most wondrous map ever produced by humankind; today we are learning the language in which God created life. We are gaining ever more awe for the complexity, the beauty, and the wonder of God's most divine and sacred gift."*

Come to Jesus with your burdens, offer them to Him, and if you have faith, you will be helped in different ways. Either they will disappear, or you will start carrying them with ease—and sometimes burdens will even turn into a glorifying purpose. Jesus will make sure to give you joy again when you invite Him to enter your heart. Francis Collins's experience resonated with me, but if you search, you will find accounts of millions of similar experiences.

Reason Two: Ask, believe, receive treats God like a genie. Many Christians agree with what Rick Warren writes in his book *The Purpose Driven Life* regarding this subject:

Many Christians misinterpret Jesus's promise of the "abundant life" to mean perfect health, a comfortable lifestyle, constant happiness, full realization of your dreams, and instant relief from problems through faith and prayer. In a word, they expect the Christian life to be easy. They expect heaven on earth. This self-absorbed perspective treats God as a genie who simply exists to serve you in your selfish pursuit of personal fulfillment. But God is not your servant, and if you fall for the idea that life is supposed to be easy, either you will become severely disillusioned or you will live in denial of reality. Why would God provide heaven on earth when he's planned the real thing for you in eternity?

Well, my answer is that no one can see the whole truth, and I respect everyone's point of view. In the end, each person sees the world from his or her unique perspective and through the lens of his or her knowledge and experience. My teaching in ask, believe, and receive is based on three pillars:

- The first pillar is based on Jesus's words. On different occasions and in different verses, Jesus has insisted that, with even a little faith we can move mountains, and if we believe when we ask, we shall receive. I will not list all the relevant verses now, because some of them are stated in the previous chapters, and the others will be mentioned in the following pages.
- The second pillar is based on my own various experiences, as listed earlier.
- The third pillar is based on what Christianity preaches. It preaches that God is the Father and we are His children. In such a relationship, I personally feel that I can ask my Father for anything I want—why not? Did Jesus define what to ask for and what not to ask for? Did Jesus limit God's blessings to a specific area of our lives? He who turned water into wine?

I will talk more later in this chapter about the Father-child relationship.

Reason Three: We don't deserve to receive. Many believe that they don't deserve to have their prayers answered, and some even believe that no one deserves God's blessings.

In a parental relationship, a child doesn't have to do a thing to earn his father's love, kindness, gifts, or forgiveness. It comes naturally. The child simply has to admit that he has a father, and exchange with him the love that the parental relationship naturally creates.

Our quest for spiritual maturity will never end. We are constantly learning. We gain spiritual growth, step by step, using meditations and prayers. We are only human, and humans make mistakes; the best of us learn from our mistakes. Because of those mistakes, however, many people feel that they aren't deserving. They forget that only God is perfection and that God is a compassionate Father.

In Luke 15:11–32, Jesus said the following:

There was a man who had two sons. The younger one said to his father, "Father, give me my share of the estate." So he divided his property between them. Not long after that, the younger son got together all he had, set off for a distant country and there squandered his wealth in wild living. After he had spent everything, there was a severe famine in that whole country, and he began to be in need. So he went and hired himself out to a citizen of that country, who sent him to his fields to feed pigs. He longed to fill his stomach with the pods that the pigs were eating, but no one gave him anything.

When he came to his senses, he said, "How many of my father's hired servants have food to spare, and here I am starving to death! I will set out and go back to my father and say to him: Father, I have sinned against heaven and against you. I am no longer worthy to be called your son; make me like one of your hired servants." So he got up and went to his father.

But while he was still a long way off, his father saw him and was filled with compassion for him; he ran to his son, threw his arms around him and kissed him. The son said to him, "Father, I have sinned against heaven and against you. I am no longer worthy to be called your son."

But the father said to his servants, "Quick! Bring the best robe and put it on him. Put a ring on his finger and sandals on his feet. Bring the fattened calf and kill it. Let's have a feast and celebrate. For this son of mine was dead and is alive again; he was lost and is found."

MY SPIRITUALITY

Christianity has provided me with a loving, parental type of relationship. In this relationship I am helped and protected by my Father and I feel peaceful and happy like never before. I feel loved and overwhelmed by

God's presence. I enjoy life, and I can freely love nature, animals, and every other human being. I feel that I am part of a beautiful universe where everything is possible, and I feel that my life on Earth is preparation for eternal life. I've learned how to enjoy the present, and being grateful for everything has made me appreciate everything. Most of all, I see the greatness of the Creator everywhere I look and in every experience I have.

I have found my purpose: to spread love, peace, and happiness and help other people achieve these as well.

How do I view this parental relationship?

In a family, parents and children have different roles. Since God is our Creator, He as a fatherly role, and we children have our role to play. Let's see what the New Testament says about both. First, I will talk about the Father's wish list and duties toward his children. Second, I will talk about how, to cement this relationship, we as children have to play our role—we have to perform certain actions and to communicate in a specific way.

SOME OF THE FATHER'S WISHES

A. Abundance

John 10:10: *The thief comes only to steal and kill and destroy; I have come that they may have life, and have it to the full.*

B. Joy

John 15:11: *I have told you this so that my joy may be in you and that your joy may be complete.*

C. Peace

John 14:27: *Peace I leave with you; my peace I give you. I do not give to you as the world gives. Do not let your hearts be troubled and do not be afraid.*

D. Happiness

John 2:1–12: *On the third day a wedding took place at Cana in Galilee. Jesus's mother was there, and Jesus and his disciples had also been invited to the wedding. When the wine was gone, Jesus's mother said to him, "They have no more wine."*

"Woman, why do you involve me?" Jesus replied. "My hour has not yet come."

His mother said to the servants, "Do whatever he tells you."

Nearby stood six stone water jars, the kind used by the Jews for ceremonial washing, each holding from twenty to thirty gallons. Jesus said to the servants, "Fill the jars with water"; so they filled them to the brim. Then he told them, "Now draw some out and take it to the master of the banquet."

They did so, and the master of the banquet tasted the water that had been turned into wine. He did not realize where it had come from, though the servants who had drawn the water knew. Then he called the bridegroom aside and said, "Everyone brings out the choice wine first and then the cheaper wine after the guests have had too much to drink; but you have saved the best till now."

What Jesus did here in Cana of Galilee was the first of the signs through which he revealed his glory; and his disciples believed in him. After this he went down to Capernaum with his mother and brothers and his disciples. There they stayed for a few days.

When I read the changing water into wine verses, I asked myself, "If there were no more wine, would that have dampened the wedding's celebration? I don't think so. Then what is the message of Jesus Christ behind this miracle that I personally see as unnecessary and materialistic when it is coming from the Son of God? The conclusion I came to is that it is God's wish to keep us happy.

God's wishes for his children are similar to the wishes that every father would want for his own children. At least from my side as a father, I wish for my children to have abundance, joy, peace, and happiness, and who wouldn't?

SOME OF THE FATHER'S DUTIES

A. The Giving Father

John 15:7: *If you remain in me and my words remain in you, ask whatever you wish, and it will be done for you.*

Matthew 7:7–11: *Ask and it will be given to you; seek and you will find; knock and the door will be opened to you. For everyone who asks receives; the one who seeks finds; and to the one who knocks, the door will be opened. Which of you, if your son asks for bread, will give him a stone? Or if he asks for a fish, will give him a snake? If you, then, though you are evil, know how to give good gifts to your children, how much more will your Father in heaven give good gifts to those who ask him!*

B. The Loving, Caring, and Forgiving Father

Luke 15:1–7: *Now the tax collectors and sinners were all gathering around to hear Jesus. But the Pharisees and the teachers of the law muttered, "This man welcomes sinners and eats with them."*

Then Jesus told them this parable: "Suppose one of you has a hundred sheep and loses one of them. Doesn't he leave the ninety-nine in the open country and go after the lost sheep until he finds it? And when he finds it, he joyfully puts it on his shoulders and goes home. Then he calls his friends and neighbors together and says, 'Rejoice with me; I have found my lost sheep.' I tell you that in the same way there will be more rejoicing in heaven over one sinner who repents than over ninety-nine righteous persons who do not need to repent."

Matthew 11:28–30: *Come to me, all you who are weary and burdened, and I will give you rest. Take my yoke upon you and learn from me, for I am gentle and humble in heart, and you will find rest for your souls. For my yoke is easy and my burden is light.*

C. Sending Guidance for Enlightenment

John 8:12: *When Jesus spoke again to the people, he said, "I am the light of the world. Whoever follows me will never walk in darkness, but will have the light of life."*

John 14:25–26: *All this I have spoken while still with you. But the Advocate, the Holy Spirit, whom the Father will send in my name, will teach you all things and will remind you of everything I have said to you.*

John 16:13–15: *But when he, the Spirit of truth, comes, he will guide you into all the truth. He will not speak on his own; he will speak only what he hears, and he will tell you what is yet to come. He will glorify me because it is from me that he will receive what he will make known to you. All that belongs to the Father is mine. That is why I said the Spirit will receive from me what he will make known to you.*

God's duties toward his children are clear in the above messages: Ask me and you'll be given. I love you, and no matter what you do. Come to me and I will forgive you. I will send you guidance to enlighten your life.

The problem with most believers is that they know what Jesus has said and promised. They want to believe, but they don't truly believe, so it isn't working. They pray for something, and it doesn't happen. They try again for something else and get no result. After trying for a while, multiple failures lead to a belief that God's words, promises, and love can be called into doubt; they keep themselves in a cycle of pain.

I used to have the same failures, and when I asked myself why, I realized that I wanted God to play the Father role, but I had never played the child role that a normal parental relationship naturally requires. There are some rules that a parental relationship dictates.

Playing the child role is simple. It is not as complicated as many people may think. Let us explore together what Jesus says about it:

PLAYING THE ROLE OF THE SON OR DAUGHTER: YOU NEED TO ACKNOWLEDGE FAMILY TIES

A. Love Your Father

Mark 12:28–30: *One of the teachers of the law came and heard them debating. Noticing that Jesus had given them a good answer, he asked him, "Of all the commandments, which is the most important?" "The most important one," answered Jesus, "is this: 'Hear, O Israel: The Lord our God, the Lord is one. Love the Lord your God with all your heart and with all your soul and with your entire mind and with all your strength.'"*

B. Love Your Sisters and Brothers and Care for Them

Mark 12:31: *The second is this: "Love your neighbor as yourself." There is no commandment greater than these.*
Matthew 7:12: *So in everything, do to others what you would have them do to you, for this sums up the Law and the Prophets.*

All that God is asking of us is to love—what do you think of that? By nature, when we are born, we seek two things in life: to be loved and to love. And this is all that God is recommending.

As a father myself, all that I want in my relationship with my children is to love them and be loved by them, and as brothers and sisters, I want them to love one another, to forgive one another, to respect and help one another, and not to harm or offend one another. This is what family is all about.

To God we are one big family, and we are all equal brothers and sisters. This is Christianity: it is the exchange of unconditional love with God and with one another. Yes, it sounds easy to achieve, but when it comes to practice "do to others what you would have them do to you," seems nearly impossible. In order to do it, there is a process of three difficult stages to go through.

Stage One: We have to eliminate our bad habits and behaviors that harm others: like anger, envy, jealousy, greed, arrogance, hatred, judgment, dishonesty, cheating, lying, superiority, ego, stealing, killing, and so on.

Stage Two (the most difficult): We have to accept and forgive others when they harm us and do bad things to us.

Stage Three: Develop more good habits and reactivate virtues like humbleness, generosity, kindness, empathy, benevolence, understanding, compassion, gratitude, truth, trust, love, and so on, and exercise them more often.

When you are in Stage Three, you are actually reactivating the virtues that your soul possessed when you were born. These are the qualities possessed by your Father, who has created you in His own image.

Please do not panic if this seems unachievable; in Part 3, "My Understanding of the Inner World," I will guide you through the process I used to cross over from Stage One to Stage Three. It is not easy, but it is not impossible.

AS A FAMILY MEMBER, YOU NEED TO DEVELOP, USE, AND CONTRIBUTE TO THE GROWTH OF THIS FAMILY BY USING YOUR TALENTS AND SKILLS

Matthew 25:14–30: *Again, it will be like a man going on a journey, who called his servants and entrusted his wealth to them. To one he gave five bags of gold, to another two bags, and to another one bag, each according to his ability. Then he went on his journey. The man who had received five bags of gold went at once and put his money to work and gained five bags more. So also, the one with two bags of gold gained two more. But the man who had received one bag went off, dug a hole in the ground and hid his master's money. After a long time the master of those servants returned and settled accounts with them. The man who had received five bags of gold brought the other five. "Master," he said, "you entrusted me with five bags of gold. See, I have gained five more."*

His master replied, "Well done, good and faithful servant! You have been faithful with a few things; I will put you in charge of many things. Come and share your master's happiness!"

The man with two bags of gold also came. "Master," he said, "you entrusted me with two bags of gold; see, I have gained two more."

His master replied, "Well done, good and faithful servant! You have been faithful with a few things; I will put you in charge of many things. Come and share your master's happiness!"

Then the man who had received one bag of gold came. "Master," he said, "I knew that you are a hard man, harvesting where you have not sown and gathering where you have not scattered seed. So I was afraid and went out and hid your gold in the ground. See, here is what belongs to you."

His master replied, "You wicked, lazy servant! So you knew that I harvest where I have not sown and gather where I have not scattered seed? Well then, you should have put my money on deposit with the bankers, so that when I returned I would have received it back with interest. So take the bag of gold from him and give it to the one who has ten bags. For whoever has will be given more and they will have abundance. Whoever does not have, even what they have will be taken from them. And throw that worthless servant outside, into the darkness, where there will be weeping and gnashing of teeth."

Matthew 6:33–34: *But seek first his kingdom and his righteousness, and all these things will be given to you as well. Therefore do not worry about tomorrow, for tomorrow will worry about itself. Each day has enough trouble of its own.*

The message is clear: Do you want to live a decent life and get rewarded? You have to be motivated, learn, and work to keep the growth flowing, using family ties as a foundation.

AS A FAMILY MEMBER I KNOW MY BENEFITS, DUTIES, AND CONTRIBUTIONS, BUT WHAT IS MY FAMILY'S GOAL?

John 3:15: *That everyone who believes may have eternal life in him.*
John 3:16: *For God so loved the world that he gave his one and only Son, that whoever believes in him shall not perish but have eternal life.*
Matthew 19:29: *And everyone who has left houses or brothers or sisters or father or mother or wife or children or fields for my sake will receive a hundred times as much and will inherit eternal life.*
Matthew 25:46: *Then they will go away to eternal punishment, but the righteous to eternal life.*

The goal is clear: We seek immortality.

HOW CAN I RETURN TO THIS FAMILY?

Jesus has shown us the way to get connected with God, that we may build with Him the Father-child relationship.

A. Awaken God within You

John 14:23–24: *Jesus replied, "Anyone who loves me will obey my teaching. My Father will love them, and we will come to them and make our home with them. Anyone who does not love me will not obey my teaching. These words you hear are not my own; they belong to the Father who sent me.*

B. Build Trust

Matthew 21:21–22: Jesus replied, *"Truly I tell you, if you have faith and do not doubt, not only can you do what was done to the fig tree, but also you can say to this mountain, 'Go, throw yourself into the sea,' and it will be done. If you believe, you will receive whatever you ask for in prayer."*

C. Communicate

Matthew 6:5–14: *And when you pray, do not be like the hypocrites, for they love to pray standing in the synagogues and on the street corners to be seen by others. Truly I tell you, they have received their reward in full. But when you pray, go into your room, close the door and pray to your Father, who is unseen. Then your Father, who sees what is done in secret, will reward you. And when you pray, do not keep on babbling like pagans, for they think they will be heard because of their many words. Do not be like them, for your Father knows what you need before you ask him.*
This, then, is how you should pray:
'Our Father in heaven, hallowed be your name,
your kingdom come, your will be done, on earth as it is in heaven.
Give us today our daily bread.
And forgive us our debts, as we also have forgiven our debtors.
And lead us not into temptation, but deliver us from the evil one.
For if you forgive other people when they sin against you, your heavenly Father will also forgive you. But if you do not forgive others their sins, your Father will not forgive your sins.

This prayer, which usually takes less than a minute to recite, takes me an hour to complete; I focus on each line as a sort of meditation.

1. *Our Father in heaven, hallowed be your name:* I smile and start listing with gratitude and enjoy the beauty that God has created in His forests, animals, us humans, the sea, the sky, the moon, the sun, and so on. I see His greatness and goodness in everything I am listing. I thank Him for giving me the blessings of life. I thank Him and the Blessed Mother for helping me believe again.
2. *Your kingdom come, your will be done, on earth as it is in heaven:* This is where the analysis of my actions and behaviors happens. How can I change a bad habit into a better one? If I have a problem that I

don't know how to solve, I ask how God would like me to solve it. What does he want me to learn? The answers to my questions will come now or later, I am certain.

3. *Give us today our daily bread:* This is where I thank Him ten times in advance for the things that I need—whether they be material, spiritual, or emotional.

4. *And forgive us our debts, as we also have forgiven our debtors:* This where I ask for forgiveness. I am weak like everyone else. I am not perfect and can never be, but that does not stop me from continuously trying. I forgive everyone who harmed or offended me; I list them by names. I also ask God to help every person I have offended, intentionally or not, and to forgive me, and I list all the names I can remember.

5. *And lead us not into temptation, but deliver us from the evil one:* I know what my temptation areas are, and I pray to God to give me strength to overcome them.

Try it—you'll see the daily changes in your life.

D. Be Thankful in Advance

Matthew 15:32–38: *Jesus called his disciples to him and said, "I have compassion for these people; they have already been with me three days and have nothing to eat. I do not want to send them away hungry, or they may collapse on the way."*

His disciples answered, "Where could we get enough bread in this remote place to feed such a crowd?"

"How many loaves do you have?" Jesus asked.

"Seven," they replied, "and a few small fish."

He told the crowd to sit down on the ground. Then he took the seven loaves and the fish, and when he had given thanks, *he broke them and gave them to the disciples, and they in turn to the people. They all ate and were satisfied. Afterward the disciples picked up seven basketfuls of broken pieces that were left over. The number of those who ate was four thousand men, besides women and children.*

John 11:38–44: *Jesus, once more deeply moved, came to the tomb. It was a cave with a stone laid across the entrance. "Take away the stone," he said.*

"But, Lord," said Martha, the sister of the dead man, "by this time there is a bad odor, for he has been there four days."

Then Jesus said, "Did I not tell you that if you believe, you will see the glory of God?"

So they took away the stone. Then Jesus looked up and said, "Father, I thank you that you have heard me. *I knew that you always hear me, but I said this for the benefit of the people standing here, that they may believe that you sent me." When he had said this, Jesus called in a loud voice, "Lazarus, come out!" The dead man came out, his hands and feet wrapped with strips of linen, and a cloth around his face. Jesus said to them, "Take off the grave clothes and let him go."*

E. Be Grateful

Matthew 13:12: *Whoever has will be given more, and they will have an abundance. Whoever does not have, even what they have will be taken from them.*

I love how Rhonda Byrne, in her book *The Magic*, explains the above verses:

You have to admit that when you read the passage it appears unjust, as it seems to be saying that the rich will be richer and the poor will be poorer. But there's a riddle to be solved in this passage, a mystery to uncover, and when you know it a new world will have opened up for you. The answer to the mystery that has eluded so many for centuries is in one hidden word: gratitude. *Whoever has gratitude will be given more, and he or she will have an abundance. Whoever does not have gratitude, even what he or she has will be taken from him or her.*

F. Don't Be Shy

Some people are too shy to ask for help from God, and others think that God is too busy and it would be a selfish act to ask Him for help. John Gray, in his book *How to Get What You Want and Want What You Have*, addresses this in the following way:

> *If you believe in God or divine energy that has infinite power, then realize there is no limit. God's power is unlimited, and there is no end to it. You cannot ask for too much, and you are never bothering God. God wants you to ask. All loving parents want to help their children. The difference between God and our parents is that God is all-powerful and unlimited.*

Let me summarize this relationship: as a Father, God loves, forgives, and helps you as his son or daughter. Your duty is to meet Him in equal measure—by believing in Him first and then by being loving, forgiving, and helping. He gave you a conscience to be able to differentiate between right and wrong. God wants you to be happy, but you have to take action and work toward it because without work and learning, there can be no growth. Know what you really want at all levels, whether in the outer, inner, or spiritual worlds, and then ask Him to help you achieve it.

12

Step-by-Step Guide to Manifestation

In this chapter, I will make the process of "ask, believe, and receive" simple to understand.

Like a satellite broadcast to all TV receivers, God's love and blessings are sent without exceptions to all His creations. If you have a TV receiver to be able receive the channel you want, you still need to set your receiver to the right satellite frequency. To be able to receive what you ask for from God, you likewise need to set your relationship to the Father-child channel frequency.

Consider these two different scenarios, both of which affect our emotions: Scenario One: You are a child with a good relationship with your father, based on trust. You communicate, you discuss, you express love, and you share your experiences with him. You are still studying at the university, your birthday is in ten days and you want the latest iPad as a gift—but you just failed your courses for the semester.

You come to your father and tell him, "Father, I failed my courses, and I know the reason—I wasn't studying enough—but I promise you that I will do my best to succeed in all my courses next semester. As you know, next week is my birthday, and I would like the latest iPad as a gift."

The questions to conisder are: A) Do you think your father should get you an iPad? B) Why or why not?

Please take a few moments and think about your answers before moving to the next scenario.

Choose one answer: Yes, he will.   I am not sure.   No, he won't.

Scenario Two: You are a child with a cold relationship with your father. You barely discuss or communicate, and you have never shared your experiences with him. You are still studying at the university, your birthday is in ten days, and you want an iPad as a gift—but you just failed your courses for the semester.

You come to your father and tell him, "Father, I failed my courses, and I know the reason—I wasn't studying enough—but I promise you that I will do my best to succeed in all my courses next semester. As you know, next week is my birthday, and I would like the latest iPad as a gift."

The questions to consider are: A) Do you think your father should get you an iPad? B) Why or why not?

Please take a few moments and give your answer.

Choose one answer: Yes, he will.   I am not sure.   No, he won't.

I have given this test to hundreds of people, and 90 percent generally answer the following:

Scenario One: Yes, my father will give me the iPad because our relationship is very good and we always communicate with each other. I feel that he trusted me when I promised him I would do better next semester.

Scenario Two: No, he won't. I am not really sure if he would because there is no communication between us, and I don't think he trusts me enough to believe my promise to him.

The moral of the story is: when you ask God for something, you should feel that you deserve it as a son and as a good person.

STEP ONE: FEELING YOU DESERVE SOMETHING

To get yourself to feel that you deserve what you have asked for, you need to follow these steps:

A. Apply Daily Prayer (Build a Father-Child Relationship)

Dedicate time, at least half an hour every day, to talk with God and pray to Him. Tell Him you want to know Him and love Him, tell Him you believe in His power and greatness, tell Him what problems you have, and ask Him to help you find a solution. Offer Him all your weaknesses and ask him to help make you stronger, and ask Him to help you be a better person. Please refer to the previous chapter, regarding why we deserve God's blessings.

B. Apply Daily Gratitude

List all the blessings you have. You have a lot of things that other people do not have. Appreciate what you do have, and be grateful for them. Count them one by one—when you do that, you will feel an overwhelming happiness.

C. Eliminate Guilty Feelings

Feeling guilty is the opposite of feeling deserving, so whatever you have on your conscience, ask God for forgiveness. If you still feel guilty, ask the person you have harmed or offended to forgive you—when you do that, you will feel relieved.

D. Exercise Forgiveness

Remember that when you forgive someone else, you are the first person to benefit from the act. If you don't forgive, negative emotions like hatred, vengeance, and anger will build up inside you. You will not sleep well, for starters. You may react in a way you might regret all your life when you are asked; meanwhile, the other person does not care about how you feel, and he or she will continue enjoying his or her life away from you. By not forgiving someone, you're actually giving that person the power to control *you*.

Matthew 6:14–15: F*or if you forgive other people when they sin against you, your heavenly Father will also forgive you. But if you do not forgive others their sins, your Father will not forgive your sins.*

The most difficult request that Jesus makes of us is in Matthew 5:43–48: *You have heard that it was said, "Love your neighbor and hate your enemy." But I tell you,* love your enemies and pray for those who persecute you, *that you may be children of your Father in heaven. He causes his sun to rise on the evil and the good, and sends rain on the righteous and the unrighteous. If you love those who love you, what reward will you get? Are not even the tax collectors doing that? And if you greet only your own people, what are you doing more than others? Do not even pagans do that? Be perfect, therefore, as your heavenly Father is perfect.*

What a difficult request! When we move to the discussion of the inner world in Part 3, I will explain to you how I succeeded in honoring this request.

If you read the above sections (A, B, C, and D) again, you will find that those acts are great sources of happiness in themselves, and they are very essential to our next step.

STEP TWO: ACT LIKE IT'S HAPPENING

A. Advance Thanking (Expectation)

You have, by now, read the chapter related to the power of thoughts and the law of attraction. And by the way, do not be afraid of science! The laws that science is discovering are laws set by the Creator himself.

Remember that everything is composed of energy and that the physical shapes we see around us are merely due to the density of that energy. As genuine as your prayers are (mind work), they need to be charged with emotions (heart work) to attract what you want.

And what is the emotion that comes from the heart to give this power?

It's the feeling that you are deserving.

This action of feeling that you are deserving puts the thought of the mind in harmony with the desire of the heart.

Now that you are set to take off, you have one simple but at the same time difficult, act to complete. It is simple because it is a single act of thanking God in advance for what you want. It is hard because your subconscious is not trained to thank someone for something that hasn't happened yet, and because believers are afraid that if it does not happen, they will lose trust in God.

B. Let God

Once your mind and heart are set to a specific need or desire, these intentions now set your direction. Your behavior sets your actions, and all the angels of God will start working to make your wish come true.

I have a colleague at work whom I respect and love very much. His original choice of vocation was to become a priest. After four years of studying, his wish was fulfilled, and he was appointed to a very beautiful village in the south. During the past four years, during our daily discussions at work, I was struggling to convince him about the advance-thanking process that helps believers cross the line from belief into faith. One day, during a mass he was giving, I was approaching the altar to participate in Communion. I was thinking about telling him to pick the biggest piece of the holy bread for me, but I couldn't bring myself to say it out loud—that would not have been appropriate, but the thought did not leave my mind. The surprise was, when I was standing in front of him, he looked purposely in the tray to find the biggest piece of the holy bread, and when he did, he gave it to me. After the mass I called him and told him what I had wished for and how it had happened.

He said, "When you were standing in front of me, my mind told me to choose the biggest piece and give it to you."

I asked, "How did it happen—how did this thought come into your mind?"

He couldn't explain it.

How many times have you thought of a friend and that friend calls you immediately or you see him or her right away? Or maybe you've wished for something, only to have it happen?

Many times, when I was stuck in my thoughts and needed answers for my seminars, I turned to books I had received as gifts or as invitations to seminars, and those books and seminars answered my questions. Many times, I was offered things I wanted. And my list of manifestations never ended.

Dear friends, believe me, when you start growing your relationship with God, you will reach the stage that Jesus promised in Matthew 6:33–34: *But seek first his kingdom and his righteousness, and all these things will be given to you as well. Therefore do not worry about tomorrow, for tomorrow will worry about itself. Each day has enough trouble of its own.*

Be careful. Do not be so emotionally attached to anything that you are blind to hearing the message of God. God talks to you through new thoughts, through someone or something, or He may close your way to divert you in a different direction.

In preparing for my seminars and workshops about the law of attraction and God's intervention, it took me years of research and meditation to come to be able to define the difference between those two and to solve this dilemma for myself:

How can I talk about science when I am talking about God? How can I mix a certain natural law with a discussion of the greatness of God?

When you use the law of attraction, you will get what you desire, but is that good for you? Does it benefit you in the long run? No one knows, because you may wish to buy a car, and you'll have it, but how would that decision affect your life or your financial position? You can't be certain.

On the contrary, whatever desire, goal, or need you ask God for, if you're in a parental relationship with him, I assure you that, if it happens, it would be for your benefit. If it does not, it was for your own good. So trust that with God you will always get what you really need. Remember Romans 8:28: *And we know that in all things God works for the good of those who love him, who have been called according to his purpose.*

C. God's Timing Is Different from Yours

Doubt and anxiety will make expectation go away. Be patient. Human time has no influence on God. God's way is unpredictable; expect what you need from unexpected sources and times.

Anthony Robbins addresses timing in his book *Awaken the Giant Within*: *"One belief that I've developed to carry me through extremely tough times is simply this: 'God's delays are not God's denials.' Often what seems impossible in the short term becomes very possible in the long term—if you persist."*

Being patient is one of the tests of faith that we all have to pass. To help you keep your patience, remember that every time you're happy, God is happier than you are. Every time you're sad, He's sad for you; therefore, He will make your happiness come true when the time is right.

D. Ask God Questions for Guidance

Every time you have problems or you're not happy, ask yourself why. And then ask God what He wants you to learn from the situation. What is the message that He is trying to make you understand?

We acquire knowledge at school by learning through quizzes and exams, and by succeeding, we pass from one level to the next. Spirituality is similar to school education; it needs to be learned, and every time you pass an exam, you go to the next level. Problems in life are essential to helping us grow in every direction. You can't stop life's problems from occurring, but every time you deal with one, it will cease to affect you anymore.

Daily self-talk during prayer—or after—is essential for our self-development and goals. It is important to know that God works in His way through you. Do not expect Him to give you the winning lotto ticket. You need to work toward the goal you have asked for—He will do the rest.

You can't expect God to give you a raise or reward unless you start looking for opportunities. When you see an opportunity, always ask yourself the following: Am I doing the right thing? Do I have other options? What do I have as an alternative? Answers will come to you through you, through people, and through circumstances, and in the end it will happen.

I quote from John Gray's book *How to Get What You Want and Want What You Have*:

> *There are some who turn it over to God, but don't get what they want in the outer world. They put it all in God's hands. This doesn't work, either. To have success, we need to do both. We need to feel responsible and ask for help. If we depend too much on God, we stop feeling our own inner wants and wishes. When things don't happen, instead of feeling disappointed, sad, or afraid, we just trust God and have faith.*
>
> *God helps those who help themselves and then ask for help. You have to do it, God only does the part that you can't do, and then God sends his angel or divine energy to help.*

Do not expect God to change other people if you do not start making the change within yourself. I will talk in Part 3, "My Understanding of the Inner World," about how the change in my inner world affected my outer world.

Now that I have given you the knowledge that's helped me so far, let's do the next exercise together.

13

Exercise: Ask, Believe, Receive

Answer the following questions using the title of each section as guidance:

Be Clear and Specific in Your Intentions

1. What do you want?

....

....

Be Certain About Your Desire

2. Why do you need it?

....

....

3. Why is it important to you?

....

....

Boost Your Emotions

4. How would your life look if you got it?

....

....

5. How would you feel if you got it?

....

....

Have No Doubt, No Worries, No Guilt

6. Do you feel you deserve it?

....

Expect the Result, and Be Confident about the Outcome

7. Why do you think you deserve it?

....

....

8. Do you feel you can do it, or that you can handle it when it comes?

....

SUGGESTED PROCESS

Every day, at least twice a day, sit quietly, relax, and focus on feeling calm inside.

1. Ask your Father verbally or by visualization for the outcome you wrote down.

2. Don't concentrate on details. Your intention should come naturally.
3. Acknowledge that the message was delivered and that your result is on the way.
4. Put a smile on your face and say ten times, "Thank You, God, for giving me [add what you asked for]?
5. Say, "I am grateful for [list what you already have]."
6. Be open to the feedback that comes to you, either inside yourself or from the environment. Realize that you triggered any and all feedback.

FEEDBACK

This last step is extremely important. Being so conditioned by a materialistic world view, we all tend to look for material results as proof of something. However, someone who wishes for wealth may actually just be desiring the security that he or she imagines wealth brings. If that need is dominant in his or her awareness, God might favor an outcome that brings a sense of security rather than material wealth. The feedback produced from an intention is capable of manifesting in unexpected ways, but some result is *always* produced, however faint it may be for us to discern.

Do not worry if you have not had much success in fulfilling your intentions in the past. Gaining clarity about the mechanics of intentions is the most important step in achieving them. By going through the exercise, you will be clearing a path to greater success; you must have complete confidence in your Creator.

When your desires don't come true, it's because your awareness has suffered some block or disconnect. Review the exercise section by section, and amend your thoughts accordingly.

There is self-referring feedback involved. In other words, every fulfilled intention teaches you how to fulfill the next intention even more smoothly. When the result occurs, it confirms the power of intention at a conscious level, increases confidence, and makes success stronger—the effect is self-reinforcing as doubt changes to certainty. (People whose desires don't come true also experience feedback, but it may reinforce failure. Be careful. Do not fall into this trap.)

14

Why Believe?

If you're living in doubt, ask God to reveal himself to you. He will. In normal relationships, love comes after people get to know one another, but with God it is the opposite; you love Him first, then get to know Him. He already loves you.

I like this story from Deepak Chopra's book *Reinventing the Body, Resurrecting the Soul*:

> *A guru was once asked by a confused disciple, "Master, how can I become a good person?"*
>
> *The guru said, "It's nearly impossible. If you think deeply, there are a thousand reasons to pick a pin up from the floor and a thousand reasons not to."*
>
> *The disciple became very worried. "Then what can I do?"*
>
> *The guru smiled. "Find God."*
>
> *Now the disciple was even more worried. "But, sir, finding God seems so far beyond my reach."*
>
> *The guru shook his head. "Finding God is a hundred times easier than trying to be good. God is part of you, and once you locate that part, being good comes naturally."*
>
> *The disciple said, "I don't believe in God."*
>
> *The teacher replied, "You will believe in God when you see him. Have you really looked?"*

The disciple blushed, taking this as criticism. "I have looked very hard, sir. I pray for God to answer me. I look for signs that He loves me. Nothing works, God might as well not exist."

The teacher shook his head. "You think God is invisible, so no wonder you don't see him. The creator is in his creation. Go into nature. Appreciate the trees, the mountains, the green meadows. Look with total love and appreciation, not superficially. At a certain point God will notice that you love his creation. Like an artist who sees someone admiring his painting, God will want to meet you. Then he will come to you, and once he does, you will believe."

God shows himself every day, to each one of us, and in a variety of forms. But God is seen only by the faithful. After the resurrection of Jesus, we are told that whenever Jesus appeared to the disciples, they did not recognize Him. When they regained their faith, then they knew they were with Him (as it happened, for example, with the two disciples of Emmaus). God shows Himself every day, but the human heart is easily closed to the knowledge of God. This is why Jesus repeats many times in the Bible, "*He who has ears, let him hear.*" He says about the Pharisees: "*They have eyes that do not see and they have ears, and hear not.*" God does not prefer to show Himself to certain people over others: He appears to everyone with an open heart.

Give it a try, believe in God, and pray to Him. What do you have to lose?

Let us next explore together the way belief is built.

What is a belief?

It's a feeling of certainty about what something means. A belief is a mental attitude that holds some proposition is true. We create beliefs to anchor our understanding of the world around us; once we have formed a belief, we will tend to persevere in that belief.

The belief formation process starts when an idea is implemented as a seed in a person's mind. This idea could be a small remark made by an authoritative person, advice given by a close friend, or even a phrase you heard from a complete stranger, certain behaviors of your role models such as teachers or parents model, or generalizations about your past based on your interpretations of painful and pleasurable experiences.

How do ideas turn into beliefs?

This happens once the idea settles into your mind, whether you want it to or not. At this point the belief is not formed yet, but as you experience different situations that cultivate it, the idea will grow and become a solid belief. The more clues a person collects to reinforce his or her inclination, the stronger the belief becomes, until it calcifies and the person believes that it's a fact that can't be changed.

I like how Anthony Robbins describes the creation of beliefs in his book *Awaken the Giant Within*:

> *Think of an idea like a tabletop with no legs. Without any legs, the tabletop won't even stand up by itself. Belief, on the other hand, has legs.* To believe something, you have references to support the idea—specific experiences that back up the belief. *These are the legs that make your tabletop solid and that make you certain about your beliefs.*
>
> *The beliefs you hold about life, yourself and people are responsible for who you are, how you behave and who you will become.*

Now that we have an idea of how a belief is created, I want to disclose the four legs that supported my belief in God and eternal life.

Support One: Jesus Christ's Life

Jesus's birth, life, words, promises, acts, miracles, and resurrection without question and without doubt do not conform to the earthly, natural laws that we can see around us.

Support Two: The Purpose of Christianity

The purpose of Christianity is immortality. What a purpose! Who wouldn't dream of having an immortal life filled with love and joy?

You might be asking yourself how you can achieve that. The answer is: by believing in God the Father and loving your neighbors as yourself.

And what is the fruit of that love and belief? The bounty is unlimited: peace, abundance, forgiveness, kindness, happiness, joy, and—I will leave it to your imagination.

Christianity gave meaning to my life, and it gave me a purpose. I now understand why so many people sacrificed their lives instead of giving up their Christian beliefs throughout the ages. And now that I know, I realize I would be ready to do the same.

Support Three: My Experience

All that I have applied from Jesus's words has given me results, just as Jesus promised. And based on that fact, I have to accept that all that He is saying about eternal life must also be true.

Support Four: Experiences of Others

John 14:12–14: *Very truly I tell you, whoever believes in me will do the works I have been doing, and they will do even greater things than these, because I am going to the Father. And I will do whatever you ask in my name, so that the Father may be glorified in the Son. You may ask me for anything in my name, and I will do it.*

In his name what we think is impossible becomes *possible*, and things that occur that we can't otherwise explain are generally called "miracles."

WHAT IS A MIRACLE?

As defined in the dictionary, a miracle derives from the Latin *mirari*, "to marvel." It indicates an event that surprises whoever witnesses it directly or indirectly. In the environment of Catholic theology, a miracle is defined as a tangible act (i.e., something that is heard, seen, touched, or experienced) performed by God through a saint, a fact that goes against, or rather beyond, common "laws" of nature as acknowledged by the particular era in which they occur.

I would like to share with you from the website www.miraclesoft-hesaints.com what others have experienced when they asked in Jesus's name:

Miracles in Healing, Curing, and Raising the Dead

Acts 9:40 states, Peter sent them all out of the room; then he got down on his knees and prayed. Turning toward the dead woman, he said, 'Tabitha, get up.' She opened her eyes, and seeing Peter she sat up.

After the disciples, the saints continued to follow Jesus's command to "heal the sick and raise the dead." Father Alfred J. Hebert, in his book Saints Who Raise the Dead, documents over four hundred true stories of resurrection miracles in the lives of the saints. Some of the many saints listed in his book are Saint Francis of Paola, Venerable John Baptist Tholomei, Saint Bernardine of Siena, and Saint Dominic.

There are also countless miraculous healings that have occurred in the lives of the saints over the centuries.

Miracles over Nature: Dogs, Birds, and Other Animals

It is absolutely amazing to see the obedience that relatively unintelligent animals often performed at the bidding of the saints. The lives of the saints are full of stories pertaining to the extraordinary influence the saints had over many different kinds of animals. God, it seems, allows the saints to have an extraordinary rapport with the animals so as to draw their fellow man closer to Him by marveling at the wonders He works between the saints and the animals.

Saint John Bosco and the mysterious dog Grigio, Saint Joseph of Cupertino and the story of the little goldfinch, Father Paul of Moll and the beautifully colored messenger birds, Saint Anthony of Padua talking to the fish and the mule, and Saint Francis of Assisi preaching to the birds, fish, rabbits, and wolves.

Prophecies in the Lives of Saints

Numerous prophecies have been recorded along with the lives of the saints throughout the course of the centuries. It seems God inspires such prophecies in the saints for the primary purpose of guiding souls closer to Him through warnings of future matters and events.

Among the countless saints known for the gift of prophecy are Saint Martin de Porres, Saint Mary Magdalene de Pazzi, Saint Francis of Paola, Saint Frances of Rome, Blessed Margaret of Castello, Saint Anthony of Padua, and Saint Bernard of Clairvaux.

Levitation Phenomena

Levitation is one of the most frequently mentioned phenomena in the lives of the saints. Many saints have experienced this marvel, including Saint Benedict Joseph Labre, Saint Angela of Brescia, Saint Antoinette of Florence, Saint Arey, Saint Peter Celestine, Saint Colette, Saint Margaret of Hungary, and Saint Martin de Porres.

Bilocation Gifts

Bilocation is a special gift from God that allows an individual to be in two places at once. God always uses this gift for acts of mercy or charity, to be performed by the saint in circumstances where it would be physically impossible for the saint to be present under normal circumstances. Probably one of the most frequent and documented accounts occurred relatively recently in the extraordinary life of the beloved Saints Padre Pio and Anthony of Padua.

OTHER GIFTS GIVEN TO JESUS CHRIST'S FOLLOWERS

- *Ability to live off the Eucharist alone for thirteen years*
- *Incorrupt bodily remains for saints*
- *Speaking in tongues—the gift of being able to be heard and understood by those of other languages*

In addition to the preceding, the saints' spirits manifest all over the world, curing people and performing miracles. The Virgin Mary's spirit is particularly known for manifesting in many different ways to people in different parts of the world.

I am fascinated by Saint Anthony of Padua. He is known as the *performer of miracles*. The variety of gifts he was given encouraged me to list some of them in detail from the website

The Mule

In the region of Tolosa, blessed Anthony, having vehemently argued about the redeeming sacrament of the Eucharist, had nearly convinced and attracted a heretic to the Catholic faith, except that, after many arguments in which he tried to back out, he added these words:

"Let's cut the chat and come to the facts. If you, Anthony, can prove with a miracle that in the Eucharist of believers there is, however hidden it may be, the true body of Christ, I will renounce every heresy and submit myself to the Catholic faith."

The Lord's servant replied with great faith: "I trust in my savior Jesus Christ that, for your conversion and for that of others, thanks to His mercy I will obtain what you ask." The heretic stood up and, asking for silence with a gesture of his hand, said: "I'll keep my beast of burden locked up for three days and I will starve him. After three days, in the presence of other people, I'll let him out and I'll show him some prepared fodder. You, on the other hand will show him what you believe to be the body of Christ. If the starving animal, ignoring the fodder, rushes to adore his God, I will sincerely believe in the faith of the Church." The saint agreed straightaway. The heretic then exclaimed: "Listen well, everyone!"

Why delay with many words? The day of the challenge arrived. People arrived from far and wide and filled up the square. Christ's servant, Anthony, was at present surrounded by a crowd of faithful and the heretic too, with a number of his accomplices. God's servant entered a

nearby chapel, to perform the rites of the Mass with great devotion. Once finished, he exited where the people were waiting, carrying reverently the body of the Lord. The hungry mule was led out of the stall, and shown appetizing food.

Finally, asking for silence the man of God said to the animal with great faith: "In the name of virtue and the Creator, who I, although unworthy, am carrying in my hands, I ask you, O beast, and I order you to come closer quickly and with humility and to show just veneration, so that the malevolent heretics will learn from this gesture that every creature is subject to the Lord, as held in the hands with priestly dignity on the altar." God's servant had hardly finished speaking, when the animal, ignoring the fodder, knelt down and lowered his head to the floor, thus genuflecting before the living sacrament of the body of Christ.

The faithful were filled with uncontrollable joy, and the heretics and nonbelievers were filled with sadness and humiliation. God was praised and blessed, the Catholic faith was honored and exalted; heretical depravity was shamed and condemned with everlasting insults. The heretic, renounced his doctrine in front of all present, and from then on was obedient to the precepts of the holy Church.

Preaching to the Fish

If intellectual men sometimes ignored his preaching, God intervened to show that he was worthy of respect, giving signs through dumb animals. In the area near Padua, there was once a group of heretics who criticized and ridiculed his preaching; the Saint went to the edge of a river, looked in the distance, and said to the heretics so that everyone would hear:

"From the moment in which you proved yourselves to be unworthy of the Word of the Lord, look, I turn to the fish, to further confound your disbelief."

And filled with the Lord's spirit, he began to preach to the fish, elaborating on their gifts given by God: how God had created them, how He was responsible for the purity of the water and how much freedom He had given them, and how they were able to eat without working.

The fish began to gather together to listen to this speech, lifting their heads above the water and looking at him attentively, with their mouths open. As long as it pleased the Saint to talk to them, they stayed there listening attentively, as if they could reason, nor did they leave their place, until they had received his blessing.

The Reattached Foot

A great miracle was caused by a confession. A man from Padua called Leonardo, once told the man of God that, among his other sins, he'd kicked his mother, and with such violence that she fell heavily to the ground.

The blessed Father Anthony, who strongly detested all wrongdoing, in the fervor of the spirit said deploringly: "the foot which kicks a mother or father should be cut off straightaway."

This simpleton, having misunderstood the sense of this phrase, and out of remorse for his ill deed and the cruel words of the Saint, rushed home and cut off his foot. The news of such a cruel punishment spread through the city, and reached God's servant. He went to the man's house straight away after an apprehensive, devout prayer, joined the cut-off foot to the leg, making the sign of the cross.

A miracle! As soon as the saint had attached the foot to the leg, tracing out the sign of the Crucifix, passing his sacred hands gently over the leg, the foot became attached to the leg so quickly, that the man stood up happily, and began to run and jump, praising God and giving infinite thanks to the blessed Anthony, who had made him sound again in such a miraculous way.

The Conversion of Ezzelino

During his tyranny, that wicked, arrogant despot, the cruel tyrant Ezzelino da Romano, had massacred an enormous number of men in Verona.

The intrepid father, as soon as he heard of this event, took the risk of meeting him in person, at his residence in the city.

He reproached him with these words:

"O enemy of God, merciless tyrant, rabid dog, how much longer will you continue to shed the blood of innocent Christians? Look, the Lord's punishment is hanging over you and it is terrible and severe!"

He said many other harsh, vehement expressions to his face. The guards were waiting for Ezzelino, as usual, to give the order to kill him. But something else happened instead, thanks to the Lord.

In fact, the tyrant, struck by the words of the man of God, lost all his ferocity and became gentle as a lamb. Then, hanging his belt around his neck, he prostrated himself before this man of God and humbly confessed his ill doings, giving the assurance that, with his consent, he would repair any wrongdoing.

He added: "Fellow soldiers, do not be surprised by this. I am telling you in all honesty, that I have seen a type of divine splendor emanating from the face of this priest, which has frightened me so much, that faced with such a terrifying vision, I had the sensation I was falling straight into hell."

From that day on Ezzelino was always very devoted to the Saint, and for as long as he lived, he restrained from the many atrocities he would have wanted to perpetrate, this according to what the tyrant himself said.

The Vision

Blessed Anthony found himself in a city to preach and was put up by a local resident. He gave him a room set apart, so that he could study and contemplate undisturbed. While he prayed by himself, in the room, the landlord continued his bustling about the house.

While he was devotedly observing the room in which Saint Anthony had immersed himself in prayer, peeping through the window, he saw a beautiful joyful baby appear in blessed Anthony's arms. The Saint hugged and kissed him, contemplating the face with unceasing attention. The landlord, awed and enraptured by the child's beauty, began to think of where such a graceful child might have come from.

That baby was the Lord Jesus. He revealed to the blessed Anthony that his host was watching. After a long time spent in prayer, the vision disappeared; the Saint called the landlord, and he forbade him from telling anyone whilst Anthony was still alive what he had seen. After the Saint passed away, the man told the tale crying, swearing on the Bible that he was telling the truth.

The Miser's Heart
In Tuscany, the great region of Italy, the funeral rites of a very rich man were being celebrated with great solemnity, as was common in these cases. At the funeral Saint Anthony was present and, moved by a sudden inspiration, began shouting that this man should not be buried in a sacred place, but outside the city walls, like a dog.

And this was because his soul was damned to hell, and the corpse was without a heart, according to the saying of the Lord, reported by Saint Luke the Evangelist: Where your treasure is, there also is your heart.

Everyone was naturally shaken at this statement, and there was a long and heated exchange of opinions. Some surgeons were called who opened the deceased's chest. But they could not find his heart, which, as the Saint predicted, was discovered in his safe with his money.

For this reason, the citizens praised the Lord and the Saint. The dead man was not buried in the prepared mausoleum, but dragged like a mule along the embankment and then buried there.

The Resurrected Young Man
In the city of Lisbon, of which Saint Anthony was a native, while his relatives were still living, that is to say his father, his mother and his brothers, two citizens were enemies and they hated each other to death. It so happened that the son of one of them, a young boy, encountered the enemy of the family, who lived near blessed Anthony's parents.

This merciless man grabbed the boy, took him home, and killed him without further ado. Then, in the deep of the night, having entered into the garden of the Saint's parents, he dug a ditch, buried the body, and fled.

As the young boy was the son of a well-known family, there was an inquest into his disappearance, and it was ascertained that the young boy had traveled through the enemy's part of town. The home and garden were therefore searched, but no clues were found. While carrying out an inspection of the garden of blessed Anthony's relatives, the boy was found, buried in the garden. For this reason, the king's executioner arrested Anthony's father and everyone else in the house, for the assassination of the boy.

Blessed Anthony, even though he was in Padua, came to know this fact through divine inspiration. That night, having obtained permission, he left the convent. While he walked during the night, he was transported miraculously to the city of Lisbon. Upon entering the city in the morning, he went to the executioner, and began to plead with him to acquit these innocent people of the accusation and set them free. But, as the man had no intention of doing such a thing, blessed Anthony ordered that the assassinated boy be brought to him.

Once the body was placed before him, he ordered the boy to rise up and say whether his relatives had killed him. The boy awoke from death and affirmed that blessed Anthony's relatives were not involved. As a result, they were exonerated and released from prison. Blessed Anthony stayed with them all day. Then, in the evening, he left Lisbon and the following morning he found himself in Padua.

To sum up, the aforementioned histories strongly support my belief.

15

Reflection on My Spiritual World

I am trying to do my best in applying various virtues to my daily life. Many times I still think and do bad things. Even though I am not perfect and I have a lot of weaknesses, I have and still experience wealth, health, love, beauty, happiness, no worries, no fears, and inner peace.

Well, I believe this is heaven on Earth, and the entrance fee is free to everyone.

Advice selected from John Gray's book *How to Get What You Want and Want What You Have* follows:

> *You prevent God's assistance and your inner power when you suppress your inner will and desire. As you grow in self-awareness and in your connection to God, the distinction between God's will and your will becomes very fine. Your power increases when your heart is open and love is flowing. At such special times, God's will becomes your will. And your will becomes one with God's will.*

A quote selected from Robin Sharma's book *The Monk Who Sold His Ferrari* follows: "*As you strive to improve the lives of others, your life will be elevated to its highest dimensions.*" This describes exactly how I feel.

The following is how Thuy Anh Le describes God's love in this beautiful presentation taken from this web page: http://slideshare.net/thuyanh_le/god-loves-you-547788:

When you say, "I can't solve this…"
God tells you, "I will direct your path." (Proverbs 3:5–6)
When you say, "It's impossible…"
God tells you, "Everything is possible." (Luke 18:27)
When you say, "I feel all alone…"
God tells you, "Never will I leave you; never will I forsake you." (Hebrews 13:5)
When you say, "I can't do it…"
God tells you, "I can do everything through Him who gives me strength." (Philippians 4:13)
When you say, "I don't deserve forgiveness…"
God tells you, "I have forgiven you." (1 John 1:9, Romans 8:1)
When you say, "I am afraid…"
God tells you, "Do not fear, for I am with you; I will strengthen you and help you." (Isaiah 41:10)
When you say, "I am tired…"
God tells you, "Come to me, all you who are weary and burdened, and I will give you rest." (Matthew 11:28–30)
When you say, "No one really loves me…"
God tells you, "I love you." (John 3:16, John 13:34)
When you say, "I don't know how to go on…"
God tells you, "I will show you the path." (Psalm 32:8)
When you say, "What path does God have for me?"
God tells you, "My beloved son Jesus Christ" (1 Timothy 2:5, Acts 4:12, John 3:16)
And when you want to know everything else that God wants to tell you…
Read the Bible (2 Timothy 3:15–17).

Part 3
My Understanding of
the Inner World

16

Nature and Nurture Influence

To understand our inner world, we need to learn what makes it think, feel, and behave in certain ways.

Many factors are involved in shaping our personality; studies show that 50 percent of our personality traits come from heredity and the rest come from the environment.

Behavioral geneticists work to discover how much of people's behavior is determined by the genetic information they inherited from their parents and how much is caused by their living conditions, learning choices, and other influences from the world around them.

For a long time, there were two schools of thought. Some scientists believed that everyone was destined to act the way they do because of the genes they inherited from their parents. These scientists believed, for the most part, that the environment that a person grew up in had little or nothing to do with the way that a person behaved. The other camp of scientists believed that humans were not inclined from birth to any certain forms of behavior. They believed that the genes children got from their parents did not matter. The environment that a child grew up in was considered the most important influence on that child's behavior.

A famous epigenetic study looked at two different strains of mice. The mice in each strain were genetically identical to one another. Normally, one strain is much smarter than the other. But then the experimenters had the mothers of the smart strain raise the babies of the dumb strain. The babies not only got much smarter, but also passed this advantage on to the next generation.

So were the mice's abilities innate or learned? The result of nature or nurture? Genes or environment?

The conclusion is that we adapt to a newly unpredictable and variable world. And we do it by developing new abilities for cultural transmission and change. Each generation can learn new skills for coping with new environments and can also pass those skills on to the next generation.

PERSONALITY TYPES ACQUIRED THROUGH HEREDITY

Learning about our personality type helps us to understand why certain areas in life come easily to us and others are more of a struggle.

According to Carl Jung's theory of psychological types, we are all different in fundamental ways. Each person's ability to process different information is limited by his or her particular "type." Jung identified sixteen hereditary types.

People could either be extroverts or introverts, depending on the direction of their activity; thinking, feeling, sensing, or intuitive, according to their own information pathways; or judging or perceiving, depending on the method by which they process received information.

Until today, most of the readings I did regarding the personality types seemed united on one point: we cannot change our basic type of personality, however, we can change the aspects of our personality that we are unhappy with by creating new beliefs and acquiring new skills and habits.

NATURE VERSUS NURTURE

Let me share with you what the American Association for the Advancement of Science Project 2061 published (http://www.project2061.org/publications/sfaa/online/chap7.htm) regarding the subject of human behavior:

Cultural Effects on Behavior

Human behavior is affected both by genetic inheritance and by experience. The ways in which people develop are shaped by social experience and circumstances within the context of their inherited genetic potential. The scientific question is just how experience and hereditary potential interact in producing human behavior.

Each person is born into a social and cultural setting—family, community, social class, language, religion—and eventually develops many social connections. The characteristics of a child's social setting affect how he or she learns to think and behave, by means of instruction, rewards and punishment, and example. This setting includes home, school, neighborhood, and also, perhaps, local religious and law enforcement agencies. Then there are also the child's mostly informal interactions with friends, other peers, relatives, and the entertainment and news media. How individuals will respond to all these influences, or even which influence will be the most potent, tends not to be predictable. There is, however, some substantial similarity in how individuals respond to the same pattern of influences—that is, to being raised in the same culture. Furthermore, culturally induced behavior patterns, such as speech patterns, body language, and forms of humor, become so deeply imbedded in the human mind that they often operate without the individuals themselves being fully aware of them.

Every culture includes a somewhat different web of patterns and meaning: Ways of earning a living, systems of trade and government, social roles, religions, traditions in clothing and foods and arts, expectations for behavior, attitudes toward other cultures, and beliefs and values about all of these activities. Within a large society, there may be many groups, with distinctly different subcultures associated with region, ethnic origin, or social class. If a single culture is dominant in a large region, its values may be considered correct and may be promoted—not only by families and religious groups but also by schools and governments. Some subcultures may arise among special social categories (such as business executives and criminals), some of which may cross national boundaries (such as musicians and scientists).

Fair or unfair, desirable or undesirable, social distinctions are a salient part of almost every culture. The form of the distinctions varies with place and time, sometimes including rigid castes, sometimes tribal or clan hierarchies, sometimes a more flexible social class. Class distinctions are made chiefly on the basis of wealth, education, and occupation, but they are also likely to be associated with other subcultural differences, such as dress, dialect, and attitudes toward school and work. These economic, political, and cultural distinctions are recognized by almost all members of a society—and resented by some of them.

The class into which people are born affects what, language, diet, tastes, and interests they will have as children, and therefore influences how they will perceive the social world. Moreover, class affects what pressures and opportunities people will experience and therefore affects what paths their lives are likely to take—including schooling, occupation, marriage, and standard of living. Still, many people live lives very different from the norm for their class.

The ease with which someone can change social class varies greatly with time and place. Throughout most of human history, people have been almost certain to live and die in the class into which they were born. The times of greatest upward mobility have occurred when a society has been undertaking new enterprises (for example, in territory or technology) and thus has needed more people in higher-class occupations. In some parts of the world today, increasing numbers of people are escaping from poverty through economic or educational opportunity, while in other parts, increasing numbers are being impoverished.

What is considered to be acceptable human behavior varies from culture to culture and from time period to time period. Every social group has generally accepted ranges of behavior for its members, with perhaps some specific standards for subgroups, such as adults and children, females and males, artists and athletes. Unusual behaviors may be considered either merely amusing, or distasteful, or punishably criminal. Some normal behavior in one culture may be considered unacceptable in another. For example, aggressively competitive behavior is considered rude in highly cooperative cultures. Conversely, in some subcultures of a highly competitive society, such as that of the United States, a lack of interest in competition may be regarded as being out of step. Although the world has a wide diversity of cultural traditions, there are some kinds of behavior (such as incest, violence against kin, theft, and rape) that are considered unacceptable in almost all of them.

The social consequences considered appropriate for unacceptable behavior also vary widely between, and even within, different societies. Punishment of criminals ranges from fines or humiliation to imprisonment or exile, from beatings or mutilation to execution. The form of appropriate punishment is affected by theories of its purpose to prevent or deter the individual from repeating the crime, or to deter others from committing the crime, or simply to cause suffering for its own sake in retribution. The success of punishment in deterring crime is difficult to study, in part because of ethical limitations on experiments assigning different punishments to similar criminals, and in part because of the difficulty of holding other factors constant.

Technology has long played a major role in human behavior. The high value placed on new technological invention in many parts of the world has led to increasingly rapid and inexpensive communication and travel, which in turn has led to the rapid spread of fashions and ideas in clothing, food, music, and forms of recreation. Books, magazines, radio, and television describe ways to dress, raise children, make money, find happiness, get married, cook, and make love. They also implicitly promote values, aspirations, and priorities by the way they portray the behavior of people such as children, parents, teachers, politicians, and athletes, and the attitudes they display toward violence, sex, minorities, the roles of men and women, and lawfulness.

Group Behavior

In addition to belonging to the social and cultural settings into which they are born, people voluntarily join groups based on shared occupations, beliefs, or interests (such as unions, political parties, or clubs). Membership in these groups influences how people think of themselves and how others think of them. These groups impose expectations and rules that make the behavior of members more predictable and that enable each group to function smoothly and retain its identity. The rules may be informal and conveyed by example, such as how to behave at a social gathering, or they may be written rules that are strictly enforced. Formal groups often signal the kind of behavior they favor by means of rewards (such as praise, prizes, or privileges) and punishments (such as threats, fines, or rejection).

Affiliation with any social group, whether one joins it voluntarily or is born into it, brings some advantages of larger numbers: the potential for pooling resources (such as money or labor), concerted effort (such as strikes, boycotts, or voting), and identity and recognition (such as organizations, emblems, or attention from the media). Within each group, the members' attitudes, which often include an image of their group as being superior to others, help ensure cohesion within the group but can also lead to serious conflict with other groups. Attitudes toward other groups are likely to involve stereotyping—treating all members of a group as though they were the same and perceiving in those people's actual behavior only those qualities that fit the observer's preconceptions. Such social prejudice may include blind respect for some categories of people, such as doctors or clergy, as well as blind disrespect for other categories of people who are, say, foreign-born or women.

The behavior of groups cannot be understood solely as the aggregate behavior of individuals. It is not possible, for example, to understand modern warfare by summing up the aggressive tendencies of individuals. A person may behave very differently in a crowd—say, when at a football game, at a religious service, or on a picket line—than when alone or with family members. Several children together may vandalize a building, even though none of them would do it on his or her own. By the same token, an adult will often be more generous and responsive to the needs of others as a member of, say, a club or religious group than he or she would be inclined to be in private. The group situation provides the rewards of companionship and acceptance for going along with the shared action of the group and makes it difficult to assign blame or credit to any one person.

Social organizations may serve many purposes beyond those for which they formally exist. Private clubs that exist ostensibly for recreation are frequently important places for engaging in business transactions; universities that formally exist to promote learning and scholarship may help to promote or to reduce class distinctions; and business and religious organizations often have political and social agendas that go beyond making a profit or ministering to people. In many cases, an unstated purpose of groups is to exclude people in particular categories from their activities—yet another form of discrimination.

The variety of personality types in addition to the diversity of the environmental factors that influence our behavior lead me to conclude the following:

1. Personality is influenced by many hereditary and environmental factors, and this makes you a unique person with a unique personality.
2. Our realization of what is right and what is wrong is based on our social world's perception. This perception is influenced by your unique personality and based on information acquired through your unique life education. Therefore, don't expect people to think, feel, behave, and act exactly like you do.

Based on the above conclusions, let's do this exercise:

Choose any person who has offended you through his or her actions or behaviors. Please take your time doing the visualizations.

*   Visualize yourself born into the person's family, having the same father and mother.

- Visualize yourself raised in the person's neighborhood.
- Visualize yourself receiving the same ethics, culture, and school education.
- Visualize yourself experiencing the same relationships.
- Visualize yourself experiencing all the person's painful and joyful emotions.

Now that you have visualized that person's life, how does it make you feel? What does your life look like? How do you perceive the world?

I am sure that through this visualization the world looks different to you. If you are this new person, would you behave and act in the same manner that the original person did when he or she offended you? Most likely: yes.

Every person you see or meet could have been you.

Many times in life, we make mistakes, we offend people, and many times we felt guilt, we wish we could go back in time and rectify the damage we did. Recall a particular time when you offended someone. What do you wish the behavior of this offended person would have been:

Crucifying you, or showing you mercy?

Hating you, or showing you forgiveness?

Understanding you, or rejecting you?

Judging you, or accepting you?

Of course what you wished is to be forgiven, to have another chance, to be accepted.

Through this exercise I learned understanding, acceptance, empathy, and forgiveness.

In my family, forgiving and asking for forgiveness are considered signs of weakness. During family reunions when uncles and aunts gather to discuss family issues, the conversation heats up whenever a member tries to prove his or her point of view. The meeting then becomes a big conflict, anger starts building up, and some think that by shouting they will be heard—the aggression of the conversion leads to each member leaving the meeting dissatisfied and offended. And since forgiving or saying sorry are not within our family culture, they end up not talking to one another for months.

At home whenever I acted against my father's will or wishes, to show me his disappointment, my father would stop communicating with me. He would wait until I asked for forgiveness, and since that act is considered a sign of weakness, I wanted to avoid it. In the end, I would wind up not talking to him for several days.

These family practices implanted in my brain several traits and beliefs:

1. Forgiveness and asking for forgiveness are signs of a weak personality.
2. Communication is not a productive way to resolve conflicts.
3. Others are expected to know and meet my expectations.

In a similar vein, let me tell you about two relationships I had that started well but ended badly.

Once, I fell in love with a girl, but the relationship was always on and off. After a while we broke up, and I was heartbroken. The breakup was due to bad communication skills, at least from my side—I expected her to know how I felt and what I wanted and to behave accordingly.

I had a close friend at the time—we didn't go a day without talking or seeing each other. If one of us had a girlfriend and wanted to invite her out, he would ask her to bring a friend with her because it seemed even dates were fun only when we were both sharing them.

Having a broken heart was too painful—I needed my best friend to be next to me for support. During this time, he was very busy at the university, and I was not a cheerful person to be with, so I ended up alone, feeling left out, disappointed, and in pain.

Based on my acquired habit, the only way I knew to communicate my disappointment to him was the way I learned at home: I stopped talking to him and avoided him for a while, thinking he would understand. Unfortunately, what I was expecting to happen did not.

Having two consecutive broken relationships was too painful, but instead of trying to learn from them about their causes and correcting them,

I created a new belief: close relationships cause pain, and I should avoid them. Therefore, I avoided close relationships. I kept a distance and did not open up to love for a long time.

After few years, I met my soul mate, Mireille, and we got married. Lucky for me, because she was patient when I stopped talking, and she communicated when I didn't. She was forgiving when I was not. I want to take this opportunity to tell her that I am so sorry for making her life difficult, and I want to thank her for saving me and for saving our marriage.

I learned only a few years ago, when I was looking for happiness, that those three virtues (communication, forgiveness, and love) can make the whole difference in relationships. They strengthen our personalities as individuals and bring us collective happiness:

- The acts of *forgiveness and asking for forgiveness* are humble acts and sources of happiness. A capacity for forgiveness is one of the most universally recognized virtues. I ask you to exercise this virtue every time you have the opportunity. It will free your heart. It will make you feel proud of yourself and happy that you're doing the right thing.
- *Communication* is a must-have skill. It is the basis of all successful (business and personal) relationships. We can't build any meaningful relationship based only on our own perceptions. The result will be deceiving. Many divorces have been caused by a difference in perception. Many business partnerships have been broken because of different visions.
- *Love, love,* and *love more,* and do it unconditionally. Do not expect any return. Open your heart, give your love in abundance, and the happier you will be. But be careful when you're in love to not turn into a possessive person.

I would like for you to visualize my life when I was exercising hatred, considering that I had been taught that asking for forgiveness was a weakness, when I could not communicate my feelings, my needs, or my expectations. My heart was closed to love. Such a pitiful situation.

17

Beliefs and Habits

My determination to be happy every moment made me more aware of my feelings and my behaviors; therefore, I concentrated my attention on the reasons behind every feeling I had.

When exploring my behaviors, I realized I had many habits—some good and some bad. Both habit types combined create a comfort zone. You don't have to reason or ask questions while you're in it. The difference between the two types is that the good habits make you feel great because you know that you are doing the right thing, and these bring you positive emotions, while the bad ones usually make you feel uncomfortable and make you lose many opportunities in life.

The question is, what is a habit, and how do you acquire it?

Based on wrong beliefs, most of my bad habits were acquired when I was young, and since then I had never questioned the validity of those beliefs that had become part of my personality.

Character basically is composed of our habits.

- A belief generates a thought.
- A thought generates an action.
- Repetitive actions create a habit.
- A habit develops a character.

Habits are powerful factors in our lives because they constantly express our character and determine whether we will be effective or ineffective in any given situation.

THE HABIT OF CRITICISM AND JUDGMENT

I don't actually remember an exact period in my life when I had low self-confidence. The reason for this was maybe the lack of my general knowledge or maybe my low self-esteem or the normal competitive traits that we all have built into us. It could have been a combination. Anyway, my belief for a long time was this: to feel good, I had to make others look bad, and the best way to accomplish this was to criticize, judge, and sometimes make fun of someone else. God knows how many people I offended. I am confident those people had a disrespectful feeling toward me. They didn't like to be around me, and some of them may have even hated me.

I also exercised criticism for any belief system that was different from my own. When I was educating myself on how to be a better person, I learned that there were two types of criticism: constructive and destructive. I also learned that criticism is necessary for making a change; destructive criticism had a negative effect, and only constructive criticism had an effect for improvement and positive change. Guess what type mine was?

I tended toward destructive criticism—why was that? Because I had the belief that to get a better result from others and to motivate them, I had to show my disappointment with anger. I had to make them feel guilty, ashamed, inadequate, irresponsible, and even stupid. When I started coaching people two years ago, I learned that many young people suffered from the effects of this destructive type of parenting. The person feels inadequate, so compensates by becoming a perfectionist in his or her work. The person is worried about how to please his or her parents and how to make them proud of him or her.

We have a duty to society to criticize bad behaviors and actions and to correct mistakes, but instead of judging people, we should only criticize their actions or behaviors in a constructive way, based on specific facts and criteria. I will tell you the truth: when I started working at showing love to my family and friends by giving constructive and positive remarks, congratulating others for what they had already achieved, giving them support, and helping them learn a better way, the results were amazing. This supportive behavior encouraged them to feel secure; they became motivated and creative and made fewer mistakes. This new belief of understanding, accepting, and caring made me feel wonderful. I felt that I was contributing to the goodness in this world—I was helping people to feel better.

THE HABIT OF FEELING IMPORTANT

If you had the chance to see me in a public place seven years ago, you would have noticed me for two reasons. First, I am a good-looking guy! Second, I would have been wearing an aggressive and angry facial expression. I believed somehow that looking angry would make other people think I was concerned about important matters, and, therefore, they would be interested in meeting me.

Who wants to socialize with a guy who looks unhappy, angry, and somehow arrogant? No one.

How stupid I was. Because of that behavior, I was not forming social connections easily, but I didn't realize this until later, when I changed my attitude into a happier one.

I have learned during my journey to find happiness about the exchange of energy. The first impression you make on people is very important. If your entrance is joyful, your positive energy will uplift other people's emotions by one level, so anytime they see you or talk about you, their memory will return to the positive energy that you once gave them—the opposite is also true. If you have an aggressive, angry look or you are arrogant, you make others lose energy and feel bad. When you're happy, you smile, and when you smile, you force others to smile. Plus, you look confident. Who wouldn't love to come over and meet you?

When I started developing a reputation for giving workshops on happiness, I had the opportunity at a gathering of 150 young boys and girls to introduce, during one hour, a four-day workshop, Coaching Happiness Toward Success. But I was not alone: there were twelve presenters, and each of us had a different subject to present. After lunch, the young attendees had to choose one subject and to register for it. Before lunch we had a mass, and the priest, the organizer of this event, gave the presenters thirty seconds to introduce themselves. How could I, in thirty seconds, introduce a four-day workshop? But with God's help, I prepared what I should say. I asked everyone to smile, and when they did, I said, "When you smile, you feel a positive emotion. That's what you will learn in the Coaching Happiness Toward Success workshop. It will help you feel this positive emotion most of the time." I went to lunch, but was anxious to find out if people would register for my introduction session. I went back to check the registration. No one was standing in front of my section, so I asked someone what was happening. The answer was that they had closed my seminar's waiting list because it had met the number of authorized enrollments after just a few minutes. I am telling you this story to reinforce the effect of a simple smile. You need only to smile to make people smile back, and you will love it—it will make your heart smile.

THE HABIT OF FEELING SUPERIOR

I tend to reject others when their thoughts and behaviors don't make sense to me. I want them to think and behave like I do because, according to my belief, *my* logic is the most sound.

Book knowledge is not enough. We must educate ourselves to be open to new beliefs. Every person has a unique personality, unique education, and unique intelligence—this will not change our way of thinking or behaving because our habits are so ingrained. We have to train our minds to accept—or at least entertain—new beliefs.

Now that I have trained myself to appreciate other perspectives, I appreciate our human uniqueness and differences more. Imagine if we all thought and wanted the same things—what would happen? We would all be a copy of one person. We need one another's differences, and if those differences are accompanied with mutual love, Earth will become heaven.

THE HABIT OF INDIFFERENCE

Hearing about someone else's problem is painful, and many times this pain is accompanied by a feeling of guilt. For a long time, I felt guilty every time I faced someone in need because I was constantly waging an internal battle between doing something to help and fleeing.

I used to hold the belief that listening to someone's problems gave me pain and wouldn't do him or her any good anyway. Surely a monetary contribution would not be enough to solve his or her problem, whatever it was, either. Therefore, I fell into the habit of escaping or closing my heart whenever I was presented with such a situation. I call this habit "indifference."

When I learned the philosophy of treating others the same way that you would want them to treat you, I opened my heart and experienced unconditional love and the joy of giving. A new habit was established: caring.

WHAT IS A HABIT?

To understand the importance of managing our habits, we must know what a habit can do and how it is created.

Here's a riddle, written by an anonymous author, that defines the characteristics of a habit:

> *I am your constant companion and at your command.*
> *I am your greatest helper or heaviest burden.*
> *I will push you onward or drag you down to failure.*
> *Show me exactly how you want something done, and in a few lessons I will do it automatically.*
> *I am the servant of all great people, and unfortunately of all failures as well. Those who are failures, I have made failures.*
> *I am not a machine, though I work with all the precision of a machine plus the intelligence of a human being.*
> *You may run me for a profit or turn me for ruin—it makes no difference to me.*

Take me, train me, be firm with me, and I will place the world at your feet.
Be easy with me and I will destroy you.

Neuroscience has now defined the association between a habit and how it affects the brain. Here is a description of this association from Anthony Robbins's book *Awaken the Giant Within*:

When we do something for the first time, we create a physical connection, a thin neural strand that allows us to re-access that emotion or behavior again in the future. Think of it this way, each time we repeat the behavior, the connection strengthens. With enough repetitions and emotional intensity, we can add many strands simultaneously; increasing the tensile strength of this emotional or behavioral pattern until eventually we have a trunk line to this behavior or feeling. This connection becomes a neural highway that will take us down an automatic and consistent route of behavior.

The neuro-association is a biological reality—it's physical. Again this is why thinking our way into a change is usually ineffective, our neuro-associations are survival tool and they are secured in our nervous systems as physical connections rather than tangible memories.

Michael Merzenich of the University of California has scientifically proven that the more we indulge in any pattern of behavior, the stronger that patterns becomes. Merzenich mapped the specific areas in a monkey's brain that were activated when a certain finger in the monkey's hand was touched. He then trained one monkey to use this finger predominantly in order to earn its food. When Merzenich remapped the touch-activated areas in the monkey's brain, he found that the area responding to the signals from that finger's additional use had expanded in size nearly 600 percent. Now the monkey continued the behavior even when he was no longer rewarded because the neural pathway was so strongly established.

An illustration of this in human behavior might be that of a person who no longer enjoys smoking but still feels a compulsion to do so. Why would this be the case? This person is physically wired to smoke. This explains why you may have found it difficult to create a change in your emotional patterns or behaviors in the past. You didn't merely "have a habit"—you had created a network of strong neuro-associations within your nervous system.

We unconsciously develop these neuron-associations by allowing ourselves to indulge in emotions or behaviors on a consistent basis. Each time you indulge in the emotion of anger or the behavior of yelling at a loved one, you reinforce the neural connection and increase the likelihood that you'll do it again. The good news is this: research has also shown that when the monkey was forced to stop using this finger, the area of the brain where these neural connections were made actually began to shrink in size, and therefore the neuro-association weakened.

This is good news for those who want to change their habits! If you'll just stop indulging in a particular behavior or emotion long enough, if you just interrupt your pattern of using the old pathway for a long enough period of time, the neutral connection will weaken and atrophy. Thus the dis-empowering emotional pattern or behavior disappears with it. We should remember this also means that if you don't use your passion it's going to dwindle.

Remember: Courage unused diminishes. Commitment unexercised wanes. Love unshared dissipates.

As you have noticed, all my habits were backed by beliefs. How did I get all these beliefs?

Anthony Robbins explains in a helpful way:

There is a conviction that events control our lives and that our environment has shaped who we are today. It's not the events of our lives that shape us, but our beliefs as to what those events mean.

What are our beliefs designed for? They're the guiding force to tell us what will lead to pain and what will lead to pleasure. Whenever something happens in your life, your brain asks two questions:

1) *Will this mean pain or pleasure?*
2) *What must I do now to avoid pain and/or gain pleasure?*

The answers to these two questions are based on our beliefs, and our beliefs are driven by our generalizations about what we've learned that could lead to pain and pleasure. These generalizations guide all of our actions and thus the direction and quality of lives.
Generalizations can:

1. *Be very useful: you look at any door handle and you believe that this door will open if you turn left or right the handle or if you push or pull. Generalizations simplify our lives.*
2. *Create limitations: Maybe you've failed to follow through on various endeavors a few times in your life, and based on that, you developed a belief that you are incompetent. Once you believe this is true, it can become a self-fulfillment prophecy.*
3. *Become limitations: for future decisions about who you are and what you're capable of.*

We must remember that most of our beliefs are generalizations about our past, based on our interpretations of painful and pleasurable experiences. The challenge is threefold:

1. *Most of us do not consciously decide what we're going to believe.*
2. *Often our beliefs are based on misinterpretation of past experiences.*
3. *Once we adopt a belief, we forget it's merely an interpretation. We treat it as a reality.*

If you want to create long-term and consistent changes in your behaviors, you must change the beliefs that are holding you back.

Beliefs have the power to create (empower) and the power to destroy (disempower): Some people have taken the pain of their past and said, because of this, I will help others. Because I was raped, no one else will be harmed again. Because I lost my son or daughter, I will make a difference in the world.

Everything you and I do, we do either out of our need to avoid pain or our desire to gain pleasure; you know you should do something, but you still don't do it. Why not? The answer is simple. At some level you believe that taking action in this moment would be more painful than just putting it off. Yet have you ever had the experience of putting something off for so long that suddenly you felt pressure to just do it, just to get it done? What happened? You changed what you linked pain and pleasure to. Suddenly, not taking action became more painful than putting it off.

The secret of success is learning how to use pain and pleasure instead of having pain and pleasure use you. If you do that, you're in control of your life. If you don't, life controls you.

Let me tell you a story. When driving home late at night, a young boy named Hadi had an accident and died. It was determined that he had been speeding while intoxicated. The pain his death caused his parents diminished when the reason for their son's death was transformed into a higher purpose—to reduce the rate of death caused by alcohol. They created a continuous awareness campaign across media sources, and they introduced a free taxi service for New Year's Eve.

THE HABIT OF BAD TEMPER

One of the bad habits I had was a bad temper. I get angry fast, and my reaction is to shout, blame, and sometimes use disrespectful words. I noticed that my bad temper and anger had four effects on me:

1. Because my anger was often a fast reaction, it would not allow me to reason or give others the chance to defend themselves. This behavior put me in a bad situation several times, especially when I was wrong at the end. And I regretted it.

2. When I was in a bad mood, all the people around me were on alert, and they would try to avoid me, avoid having any discussions with me, or even to see me.
3. People did what I asked them to do not because they respected me or because I was their senior but out of fear, and this made me feel unrespected.
4. Every time I got angry and used my bad temper, even though this feeling energized me, it killed my inner peace, and it made me unhappy.

Becoming aware of the bad effects my temper had on me and my environment was when I decided to stop. The first step in changing a habit is to create a new belief.

Stopping a habit I'd exercised for many years was not an easy task. I started the process by noticing when something upset me. Before acting on that upset, I started counting from one to ten. The counting gave time for my reason to take control. For a few weeks, I would only reach one or two before my anger took control. After about six months, however, I was able to let my reason act. Now, staying cool is a new habit that's replaced the bad temper.

If you have a bad temper, find out what is causing it. It is called an *emotional hijack* and it can be cured.

Many people acquire this habit due to accumulated stress; analyze the reason for your hidden anger, change your belief, and create new habits. Keep reading to learn how.

WHAT IS AN EMOTIONAL HIJACK?
Emotional Hijack Characterization

- When people jump into action purely based on their feelings (their actions are usually inappropriate because they are based only on "partial" information);
- When people withdraw, shut down, or become extremely aggressive before they have the chance to analyze a situation logically and think things through;

- When, post event, people find it difficult to explain why they did what they did and come to regret it;
- When a person's reaction has a strong impact on him or her and those around that person.

Now let's have a look at the major parts of the brain. The brain consists of the following main three parts:

Reptilian brain: Controls basic functions of the body, such as heart rate, breathing, temperature control, digestion, and so on.

Mammalian brain (limbic brain): Takes care of functions such as sexuality, instincts, emotions, immune system, blood pressure, blood sugar, and so on. It contains the amygdala, which is responsible for our emotional processing, as well as the hypothalamus, thalamus, and hippocampus. These play a critical role in long-term memory and spatial navigation.

Cerebral cortex: Processes visual, auditory, and kinesthetic data and is responsible for reasoning and intellectual processes. It also compares previous memories with new situations so the body can react accordingly.

The discovery of the role of the amygdala in our behavior is relatively recent. Daniel Goleman explained the significant breakthroughs in the field of neuroscience and the role of the amygdala in his best-selling books *Emotional Intelligence* and *Working with Emotional Intelligence*. A lot of this research originated with the great work carried out by Joseph LeDoux, a neuroscientist at New York University.

The conventional view held by neuroscientists about how the brain processes information is that the sensory information is first passed to the thalamus, in the mammalian part of the brain, and from there it is sent to the visual cortex, which processes the information and compares it with your world model, and, eventually, you identify the objects you see or are experiencing. From there the signals are sent to the limbic brain, and commands are then sent to the rest of the body to generate an appropriate behavior.

In fact this is the way our brain works *most of the time* as we perceive the world, evaluate it, and respond to it. However, LeDoux found something remarkable: there is a smaller bundle of neurons connecting the thalamus to the amygdala. This small pathway allows the amygdala to receive a selection of sensory information coming in before it has been sent to the visual cortex for further processing. In other words, the amygdala can receive information and formulate a quick response well before the rest of the brain has processed the situation. This discovery explains a lot about our fight-or-flight behavior, quick emotional reactions to novel situations, and our built-in hardwired system that is capable of short-circuiting our logical mind. No wonder we can sometimes be so vulnerable!

The emotional hijack has four stages:

1. *Identify a trigger*—an event that is registered by you as a threat.
2. *Feel a strong emotion*—you suddenly *feel* different as a result of the trigger.
3. *Have an automatic reaction*—you automatically respond based on the trigger and the emotion you feel. It is likely that you will regret your reaction later on, which can have a negative effect on you and others.
4. *Experience regret*—this is a feeling of regret about your reaction.

WHEN ARE HIJACKS MOST LIKELY?

- When you are feeling tired;
- When you have accumulated stress in the past few days or weeks;
- When you have been drinking alcohol;
- When you have been involved in something you believe in strongly and care about a lot;
- When you have been involved in something significant and have invested a lot of effort.

HOW CAN YOU AVOID AN EMOTIONAL HIJACK?

With a short-circuiting amygdala, you need to look at the triggers that start the process and lead to your quick reactions. You can monitor your emotions and train yourself to quickly respond to specific triggers that lead to emotional behaviors. By recognizing the triggers, you can attempt to filter the data and effectively eliminate your automatic responses.

Now let's examine the stages of emotional hijacking:

First, you receive triggers when you are not feeling emotionally intense.

What happens next?

You respond to this trigger and present a *reaction*.

- Physical response: holding breath, increased heart rate
- Feelings: fear, anger
- Automatic reaction: shouting, smashing, running away

The reaction can be highly emotional, which may lead to another, even more intense, state. What do you think that is? Regret.

How can you improve this situation?

As soon as the trigger is received, you react to the trigger by recognizing that you are about to be hijacked. You can then take more appropriate actions to calm yourself down or to artificially impose a delay on yourself so your logical brain has time to catch up. It is commonly advised that if you get angry, you should count to ten before saying anything.

BELIEF CAPACITY

Anthony Robbins shares the following in his book *Awaken the Giant Within:*

Beliefs even have capacity to override the impact of drugs on the body. While most people believe that drugs heal, studies in the new science of psychoneuroimmunology (the mind-body relationship) have begun to bear out what many others have suspected for centuries: our beliefs about the illness and its treatment play as significant a role, maybe even more significant role, than the treatment itself. Dr. Henry Beecher from Harvard University has done extensive research that clearly demonstrates that we often give credit to a drug, when in reality it's the patient's belief that makes the difference. One demonstration of this was a groundbreaking experiment in which one hundred medical students were asked to participate in testing two new drugs. One was described to them as a super-stimulant in a red capsule, the other as a super-tranquilizer in a blue capsule. Unknown to the students, the contents of the capsules had been switched: the red capsule was actually a barbiturate, and the blue capsule was actually an amphetamine. Yet half of the students developed physical reactions that went along with their expectations—exactly the opposite of the chemical reaction the drugs should have produced in their bodies! These students were not just given placebos; they were given actual drugs. But their beliefs overrode the chemical impact of the drug on their bodies. As Dr. Beecher later stated, a drug's usefulness "is a direct result of not only the chemical properties of the drug, but also the patient's belief in the usefulness and effectiveness of the drug."

HOW TO BREAK AN UNDESIRABLE BEHAVIOR

Start analyzing your behavior based on the behavior cycle that follows, because many beliefs are created through this cycle:

A. My self-esteem influences my behavior.

B. People only see my behavior.

C. People react to my behavior.

D. People develop opinions about me.

E. Their opinions lead to their behavior toward me.

F. Their behavior influences my self-esteem.

When you are not feeling confident, you project uncertainty. This lack of confidence will be noticed by others. For example, your uncertainty over something may make others less sure of your intentions. This, in turn, can affect their confidence in what you are talking about. When their confidence in what you are saying is affected, it can be reflected in *their* behavior. They may stop listening, feel that their time is being wasted, or not be easily convinced by you. When you observe this behavior, it affects *your* self-esteem. You may wonder why these people are not listening to you. Perhaps you are just not that interesting! A destructive self-talk can start, which could make you feel a lot worse.

How does this lead to a vicious cycle? As each cycle reduces your self-esteem, another person's behavior changes toward you, which, in turn, reduces your self-esteem even further. Naturally, this negative cycle is very destructive.

Can this be changed to some other type of cycle? Yes, it can be turned into a virtuous cycle. If you feel confident, others will pay more attention and, through their behavior, let you know that they like to listen to you. This, in turn, boosts your self-esteem and leads to a better performance the next time.

What does the behavior cycle suggest? In summary, our behavior toward others can have a direct impact on our own emotional state, and our emotional state has a direct impact on our behavior.

Sometimes, as you are talking to a few people, you might see two of those people start talking to each other. Others enter into their conversation. You may wonder if anyone is still listening to you.

If this happens frequently, it may dramatically affect your self-confidence.

To break this cycle, you must start by noticing your behavior. If it is caused by your belief of your self-esteem, change the belief—it will influence your behavior and actions.

HOW TO BREAK A BAD HABIT

First, create a new belief to replace the one causing the habit you want to break.

Second, create a new habit to replace the present one, based on the new belief (the new habit could be to stop doing the present habit).
Answer the following questions:

1a. What habit do I want to break?
....

1b. What belief causes this habit?
....

2a. Why do I need this habit to change?
....

2b. Why is that important to me?
....

3a. What is the new belief that I want to replace the present one?
....

3b. What is the new habit that I want to replace the present one?
....

4a. What should my life look like if I get this new habit implanted?
....

4b. How should I feel if I get it?
....

5a. Do I have enough knowledge about this new belief?
....

5b. Do I have the skills, the know-how, that this new habit requires?
....

- Notice the trigger that activates this habit.
- Every time the trigger is on, count from one to ten before taking any action (when you first start out, you won't be able to count—your habit is faster than your reason).
- Repeat the noticing and the counting until your reason takes control.
- Keep repeating until it becomes a habit.

As Paulo Coelho said, *"If you conquer yourself, then you conquer the world."*

18

Values

Beliefs have the power to create, or empower, and the power to destroy, or disempower.

The following story, taken from the web page http://academictips.org/blogs/the-elephant-rope/ describes how disempowering beliefs are:

> *An observer was passing by some elephants, suddenly stopped, confused by the fact that these huge creatures were being held by only a small rope tied to their front leg. No chains, no cages. It was obvious that the elephants could, at any time, break away from the ropes they were tied to, but for some reason, they did not. He saw a trainer nearby and asked why these beautiful, magnificent animals just stood there and made no attempt to get away.*
>
> *"Well," the trainer said, "when they are very young and much smaller we use the same size of rope to tie them and, at that age, it's enough to hold them. As they grow up, they are conditioned to believe they cannot break away. They believe the rope can still hold them, so they never try to break free."*

These animals could, at any time, break free from their bonds, but because they believed they couldn't, they were stuck right where they were.

Like the elephants, how many of us go through life hanging onto the belief that we are not able to do a task or a job simply because we failed at it once before?

How many of us are being held back by old, outdated beliefs that no longer serve us?

How many of us have avoided trying something new because of a limiting belief?

Worse, how many of us are being held back by someone *else's* limiting beliefs?

How do you know if a belief is empowering? You know that a belief is empowering you when it allows you to apply your values to your life.

Anthony Robbins shares the following in his book *Awaken the Giant Within*:

> *Values guide our decision and, therefore, our destiny. Those who know their values and live by them become the leaders of our society.*
>
> *If you've ever found yourself in a situation where you had a tough time making a decision about something, the reason is that you weren't clear about what you value most within that situation. When you know what's most important to you, making a decision is quite simple.*
>
> *Your values are the compass that is guiding you to make certain decisions and take certain actions consistently. Not using your internal compass intelligently results in frustration, disappointment, lack of fulfillment. On the other hand there's an unbelievable power in living your values, a sense of certainty, an inner peace, a total congruency that few people ever experience.*

Martin Seligman shares the following in his book *Authentic Happiness*:

> *Virtues serve you best not when life is easy, but when life is difficult. The strengths and virtues function to buffer against misfortune and against the psychological disorders.*
>
> *Building strength and virtues and using them in daily life are very much a matter of making choices. Building strength and virtues is not about learning, training, or conditioning, but about discovery, creation, and ownership.*

We talked about empowering values, but what are they? There are more than a thousand character traits. Martin Seligman and his team of psychologists and psychiatrists have selected six core virtues and twenty-four strengths. To be considered a strength, a trait must include these three criteria:

1. They are valued in almost every culture.
2. They are valued in their own right, not just as a means to other ends.
3. They are malleable.

Following are the selected six core virtues:

1. Wisdom and knowledge
2. Courage
3. Love and humanity
4. Justice
5. Temperance
6. Spirituality and transcendence

Following are the twenty-four strengths. Their descriptions are taken from the handbook *Character Strengths and Virtues* by Christopher Peterson and Martin Seligman.

WISDOM AND KNOWLEDGE

1. Creativity (originality, ingenuity)
Thinking of novel and productive ways to do things; includes artistic achievement but is not limited to it
Creativity, ingenuity, and originality: Thinking of new ways to do things is a crucial part of who you are. You are never content with doing something the conventional way if a better way is possible.

2. Curiosity (interest, novelty-seeking, openness to experience)

Taking an interest in all of ongoing experience for its own sake; finding subjects and topics fascinating; exploring, and discovering

Curiosity and interest in the world—You are curious about everything. You are always asking questions, and you find all subjects and topics fascinating. You like exploration and discovery.

3. Open-Mindedness (judgment, critical thinking)

Thinking things through and examining them from all sides; not jumping to conclusions; being able to change one's mind in light of evidence; weighing all evidence fairly

Judgment, critical thinking, and open-mindedness—Thinking things through and examining them from all sides are important aspects of who you are. You do not jump to conclusions, and you rely only on solid evidence to make your decisions. You are able to change your mind.

4. Love of Learning

Mastering new skills, topics, and bodies of knowledge, whether on one's own or formally; obviously related to the strength of curiosity but goes beyond it to describe the tendency to add systematically to what one knows

Love of learning—You love learning new things anywhere and everywhere there is an opportunity to learn.

5. Perspective (wisdom)

Being able to provide wise counsel to others; having ways of looking at the world that make sense to oneself and to other people

Perspective (wisdom)—Although you may not think of yourself as wise, your friends hold this view of you. They value your perspective on matters and turn to you for advice. You have a way of looking at the world that makes sense to others and to yourself.

COURAGE

6. Bravery (valor)

Not shrinking from threat, challenge, difficulty, or pain; speaking up for what is right even if there is opposition; acting on convictions even if unpopular; includes physical bravery but is not limited to it

Bravery and valor—You are a courageous person who does not shrink from threat, challenge, difficulty, or pain. You speak up for what is right even if there is opposition. You act on your convictions.

7. Persistence (perseverance, industriousness)

Finishing what one starts; persisting in a course of action in spite of obstacles; "getting it out the door"; taking pleasure in completing tasks

Industry, diligence, and perseverance—You work hard to finish what you start. No matter the project, you "get it out the door" in a timely fashion. You do not get distracted when you work, and you take satisfaction in completing tasks.

8. Integrity (authenticity, honesty)

Speaking the truth but more broadly presenting oneself in a genuine way; being without pretense; taking responsibility for one's feelings and actions

Honesty, authenticity, and genuineness—You are an honest person, not only by speaking the truth but by living your life in a genuine and authentic way. You are down to earth and without pretense; you are a "real" person.

LOVE AND HUMANITY

9. Vitality (zest, enthusiasm, vigor, energy)

Approaching life with excitement and energy; not doing things halfway or halfheartedly; living life as an adventure; feeling alive and activated

Zest, enthusiasm, and energy—Regardless of what you do, you approach it with excitement and energy. You never do anything halfway or halfheartedly. For you life is an adventure.

10. Love

Valuing close relations with others, in particular those with whom sharing and caring are reciprocated; being close to people

Capacity to love and be loved—You value close relations with others, in particular those with whom sharing and caring are reciprocated. The people to whom you feel most close are the same people who feel most close to you.

11. Kindness (generosity, nurturance, care, compassion, altruistic love, "niceness")

Doing favors and good deeds for others; helping them; taking care of them; kindness and generosity

You are kind and generous to others, and you are never too busy to do a favor. You enjoy doing good deeds for others, even if you do not know them well.

JUSTICE

12–13. Citizenship (social responsibility, loyalty, teamwork)

Working well as a member of a group or team; being loyal to the group; doing one's share

Citizenship, teamwork, and loyalty—You excel as a member of a group. You are a loyal and dedicated teammate, you always do your share, and you work hard for the success of your group.

14. Fairness

Treating all people the same according to notions of fairness and justice; not letting personal feelings bias decisions about others; giving everyone a fair chance

Fairness, equity, and justice—Treating all people fairly is one of your abiding principles. You do not let your personal feelings bias your decisions about other people. You give everyone a chance.

15. Leadership
Encouraging a group of which one is a member to get things done and at the same time maintain good relations within the group; organizing group activities and seeing that they happen

> *Leadership—You excel at the tasks of leadership: encouraging a group to get things done and preserving harmony within the group by making everyone feel included. You do a good job organizing activities and seeing that they happen.*

TEMPERANCE

16. Forgiveness and Mercy
Forgiving those who have done wrong; giving people a second chance; not being vengeful
> *Forgiveness and mercy—You forgive those who have done you wrong. You always give people a second chance. Your guiding principle is mercy and not revenge.*

17. Humility and Modesty
Letting one's accomplishments speak for themselves; not seeking the spotlight; not regarding one's self as more special than one is
> *Modesty and humility—You do not seek the spotlight, preferring to let your accomplishments speak for themselves. You do not regard yourself as special, and others recognize and value your modesty.*

18. Prudence *Occasionally*
Being careful about one's choices; not taking undue risks; not saying or doing things that might later be regretted

Caution, prudence, and discretion—You are a careful person, and your choices are consistently prudent ones. You do not say or do things that you might later regret.

19. Self-Regulation (self-control)
Regulating what one feels and does; being disciplined; controlling one's appetites and emotions

Self-control and self-regulation—You self-consciously regulate what you feel and what you do. You are a disciplined person. You are in control of your appetites and your emotions, not vice versa.

SPIRITUALITY AND TRANSCENDENCE

20. Appreciation of Beauty and Excellence (awe, wonder, elevation)
Noticing and appreciating beauty, excellence, and skilled performance in all domains of life, from nature to art to mathematics to science to everyday experience

Appreciation of beauty and excellence—You notice and appreciate beauty, excellence, and skilled performance in all domains of life, from nature to art to mathematics to science to everyday experience.

21. Gratitude
Being aware of and thankful for the good things that happen; taking time to express thanks

Gratitude—You are aware of the good things that happen to you, and you never take them for granted. Your friends and family members know that you are a grateful person because you always take the time to express your thanks.

22. Hope (optimism, future-mindedness, future orientation)
Expecting the best in the future and working to achieve it; believing that a good future is something that can be brought about

Hope, optimism, and future-mindedness—You expect the best in the future, and you work to achieve it. You believe that the future is something that you can control.

23. Humor (playfulness)

Liking to laugh and tease; bringing smiles to other people; seeing the light side; making (not necessarily telling) jokes

Humor and playfulness—You like to laugh and tease. Bringing smiles to other people is important to you. You try to see the light side of all situations.

24. Spirituality (religiousness, faith, purpose)

Having coherent beliefs about the higher purpose and meaning of the universe; knowing where one fits within the larger scheme; having beliefs about the meaning of life that shape conduct and provide comfort

Spirituality, sense of purpose, and faith—You have strong and coherent beliefs about the higher purpose and meaning of the universe. You know where you fit in the larger scheme. Your beliefs shape your actions and are a source of comfort to you.

There is a truth that we must know about virtues. This truth is shared in Stephen Covey's book *The 7 Habits of Highly Effective People*:

They are part of most every major enduring religion, as well as enduring social philosophies and ethical systems. They are self-evident and can be easily validated by any individual, it's almost as if they are part of the human condition, part of the human consciousness, part of the human conscience, they seem to exist in all human beings. When you apply them, you know that you're doing the right thing and in that sense you are in control. If not, you have to pay the price in a sense that you're not in control.

Let us name the package of the twenty-four values "Values Principle" to facilitate the next examples of using values in our life.

Stephen Covey continues:

Each person has a center (the driving force), though we usually don't recognize it as such, that center comprised of our basic paradigms, the lens through which we see the world.

Let us examine several centers or core paradigms people typically have:

1. *Spouse centeredness*
2. *Family centeredness*
3. *Money centeredness*
4. *Work centeredness*
5. *Possession centeredness*
6. *Pleasure centeredness*
7. *Friend/enemy centeredness*
8. *Self-centeredness*
9. *Principle centeredness*

These are some of the more common centers from which people approach life. It is often much easier to recognize the center in someone else's life than to see it in your own. You probably know someone who puts making money ahead of everything else and someone whose energy is devoted to justifying his or her position in an ongoing negative relationship. If you look, you can sometimes see beyond behavior into the center that creates it.

Spouse centeredness
If our sense of emotional worth comes primarily from our marriage, then we become highly dependent upon that relationship, we become vulnerable to the moods and feeling, the behavior and treatment of our spouse, or to any external event that may impinge on the relationship—a new child, in-laws, economic setbacks, social success, and so forth.

Family centeredness

People who are family centered get their sense of security of personal worth from the family tradition and culture or the family reputation. Thus they become vulnerable to any changes in that tradition or culture and to any influences that would affect that reputation.

Money centeredness

Another logical and extremely common center to people's lives is making money. Economic security is basic to one's opportunity to do much in any other dimension. In a hierarchy or range of needs, physical survival and financial security comes first. Other needs are not even activated until that basic need is satisfied, at least minimally. When my sense of personal worth comes from my net worth, I am vulnerable to anything that will affect that net worth. But work and money provide no wisdom, no guidance, and only a limited degree of power and security. All it takes to show the limitations of a money center is a crisis in my life or in the life of a loved one. Money-centered people often put aside family or other priorities, assuming everyone will understand that economic demands come first.

Work centeredness

Work-centered people may become "workaholics," driving themselves to produce at the sacrifice of health, relationships, and other important areas of their lives. Their fundamental identity comes from their work; therefore their security is vulnerable to anything that happens to prevent them from continuing in it. Their guidance is a function of the demands of the work. Their wisdom and power come from the limited areas of their work, rendering them ineffective in other areas of life.

Possession centeredness

A driving force of many people is possessions—not only tangible, material possessions such as fashionable clothes, homes, cars, boats, and jewelry, but also the intangible possessions of fame, glory, or social prominence. Most of us are aware, through our own experience, how singularly defective such a center is, simply because it can vanish rapidly and it is influenced by so many forces. If my sense of security lies in my reputation or in the things I have, my life would be in a constant state of threat and jeopardy that these possessions may be lost or stolen or devalued. If I'm in the presence of someone of greater net worth or fame or status, I feel inferior. If I'm in the presence of someone of lesser net worth or fame or status, I feel superior. My sense of self-worth constantly fluctuates. I don't have any sense of constancy or anchorage or persistent selfhood. I am constantly trying to protect and insure my assets, properties, securities, position, or reputation. We all heard stories of people committing suicide after losing their fortunes in a significant stock decline or their fame in a political reversal.

Pleasure centeredness

Innocent pleasure in moderation can provide relaxation for the body and mind and can foster family and other relationships. But pleasure, per se, offers no deep, lasting satisfactions or sense of fulfillment. The pleasure-centered person, too soon bored with each succeeding level of "fun," constantly cries for more and more. So the next new pleasure has to be bigger and better, more exciting, with a bigger "high." A person in this state becomes almost entirely narcissistic (in love with oneself) interpreting all of life in terms of the pleasure it provides to the self here and now.

Friend/Enemy centeredness

Young people are particularly, though certainly not exclusively, susceptible to becoming friend-centered. Acceptance and belonging to a peer group can become almost supremely important. The distorted and ever-changing social mirror becomes the source for the four life-support factors, creating a high degree of dependence on the fluctuating moods, feelings, attitudes and behavior of others. Friend centeredness can also focus exclusively on one person, taking on some of the dimensions of marriage. The emotional dependence on one individual, the escalating need/conflict spiral, and the resulting negative interactions can grow out of friend centeredness.

And what about putting an enemy at the center of one's life? Most people would never think of it, and probably no one would ever do it consciously. Nevertheless, enemy centering is very common, particularly when there is frequent interaction between people who are in real conflict. When someone feels he has been unjustly dealt with by an emotionally or socially significant person, it is very easy for him to become preoccupied with the injustice and make the other person the center of his life; the enemy-centered person is counterdependently reacting to the behavior and attitude of a perceived enemy.

Self-centeredness

Perhaps the most common center today is the self. The most obvious form is selfishness, which violates the values of most people. But if we look closely at many of the popular approaches to growth and self-fulfillment, we often find self-centering at their core.

Values Principle Center

Our security *comes from knowing that, unlike other centers based on people or things, which are subject to frequent and immediate change, correct principles do not change. We can depend on them.*

Even in the midst of people or circumstances that seem to ignore the principles, we can be secure in the knowledge that principles are bigger than people or circumstances, and that thousands of years have seen them triumph, time and time again. Even more important, we can be secure in the knowledge that we can validate them in our own lives, by our own experience.

The personal power *that comes from principle-centered living is the power of a self-aware, knowledgeable, proactive individual, unrestricted by the attitudes, behaviors, and actions of others or by many of the circumstances and environment influences that limit other people.*

The only real limitation of power is the natural consequences of the principles themselves. We are free to choose our actions, based on our knowledge of correct principles, but we are not free to choose the consequences of those actions. Remember, if you pick one end of the stick, you pick up the other.

Principles always have natural consequences attached to them. There are positive consequences when we live in harmony with the principles and negative consequences when we ignore them. But because these principles apply to everyone, whether or not they are aware, this limitation is universal. And the more we know of correct principles, the greater is our personal freedom to act wisely.

By centering our lives on timeless, unchanging principles, we create a fundamental paradigm of effective living. It is the center that puts all other centers in perspective.

Remember that your paradigm is the source from which your attitudes and behaviors flow. A paradigm is like a pair of glasses; it affects the way you see everything in your life. If you look at things through the paradigm of correct principles, what you see in life is dramatically different from what you see through any other centered paradigm.

When you validate the values principle, each value will become a belief, and each belief will empower you more.

19

Map

Talking about values, beliefs, and habits is a great thing. We know what empowers us. We know how to change our bad habits. We know the influence of our culture and genes on our personality. But where do we start?

For this great knowledge to become executable, we need to create a map. Let us call this map the *mission statement*.

The mission statement will guide you toward your goals and fulfillment. It will help you correct your beliefs, prioritize what you want, and exercise your strength and values principle.

My mission statement looks like this:

- Trust and love God.
- Exercise gratitude many times a day.
- Live by integrity, honesty, trustworthiness, transparency, love, forgiveness, caring, and helping.
- Fulfill my joyful role, commitment, and responsibilities as a husband and as a father.
- Lead by example.
- Make the world a better place by spreading peace, love, and happiness.
- Preach Jesus's words, as they are the sources of all virtues.
- Develop my knowledge and self-awareness.
- Maintain financial and spiritual growth.

I have selected the following guidelines to help you create your own personal mission statement form from: www.timethoughts.com/goalsetting/mission-statements.htm:

WRITING A PERSONAL MISSION STATEMENT

- *Keep it simple, clear, and brief. The best mission statements tend to be three to five sentences long.*
- *Your mission statement should touch upon what you want to focus on and who you want to become as a person (your character) in this part of your life. Think about specific actions, behaviors, habits, and qualities that would have a significant positive impact in this part of your life over the next one to three years.*
- *Make sure your mission statement is positive. Instead of saying what you don't want to do or be, say what you do want to do or be. Find the positive alternatives to any negative statements.*
- *Include positive behaviors, character traits, and values that you consider particularly important and want to develop further.*
- *Think about how your actions, habits, behaviors, and character traits in this area affect the important relationships in your life.*
- *Create a mission statement that will guide you in your day-to-day actions and decisions. Make it a part of your everyday life.*
- *Think about how your mission affects the other areas of your life. Is it consistent with your other personal mission statements? Will it conflict with or contradict something else? Is it balanced?*
- *Make it emotional. Including an emotional payoff in your mission statement infuses it with passion and will make it even more compelling, inspiring, and energizing.*

Remember that your mission statement is not cast in stone. It will continue to change and evolve as you gain insights about yourself and what you want out of each part of your life.

20

Paradigm Shift

Mother Teresa said, "*I will never attend an antiwar rally. If you have a peace rally, invite me.*"

She understood the secret of positive thinking. Look what she manifested in the world!

Everything you experience in your life is merely a fact. The negative emotions you attach to those facts, however, are what keep you from reaching your goals and being happy.

There are several techniques for changing the negative emotions that a situation or problem can engender in you, and each technique can work in a particular situation:

1. POSITIVE SELF-TALK

Statistics say that 90 percent of what we worry about never happens; therefore, if I am not worried, I stop having negative thoughts. I start counting my blessings, and that will help me regain my belief in God, who is supporting me all the time, as I testified earlier in the "Ask, Believe, Receive" chapter.

Difficult experiences have forged my character.

I use every problem as an opportunity to learn; therefore, in every difficult situation, I ask myself what virtue I am being presented with learning. I believe that part of my spiritual development was learning values—the more values I learned, the better person I became, and the closer to God I felt.

Learn how to build on your strengths. If you don't know how to do that by yourself, find a life coach who can help you move forward, to where you want to go. As Martin Seligman says in his book *Authentic Happiness*, *"The best therapists do not merely heal damage; they help people identify and build their strengths and their virtues. Cognitive therapy for depression developed as a technique to free people from their unfortunate past by getting them to change their thinking about the present and the future."*

2. CHANGING ROLES CAN AFFECT THE WAY WE SEE THINGS

When I change my role, I need to learn to understand my opponent(s)—partner, colleagues, and children.

I have used this step in my work many times to understand what my superiors and my colleagues expect me to deliver. It's a self-motivating step. I suggest you read the inspiring book *The Leader Who Had No Title* by Robin Sharma.

While parenting, I used to remind myself of my own behavior when I was my child's age, and that helped me understand his behavior and needs.

I learned gender intelligence. I put myself in my wife's role and tried to imagine and feel what she needed and what I could do to make her happy—and did it. She's happy, and her happiness makes *me* happy.

3. CHANGE OF FOCUS

The technique of transforming your emotional association to the facts of daily life involves changing the way you see those facts from negative to positive.

BABOON STORY

When your mind is trapped on one issue and you feel only negative feelings like worry, fear, anger, hatred, blame, guilt, and so on, and you cannot let go, you have to redirect your focus to something positive. To illustrate that, I have chosen a story from Deepak Chopra's book *Reinventing the Body, Resurrecting the Soul*:

There are clever tactics reputedly used by the indigenous bushmen of South Africa to find water. In the desert regions that the Bushmen have long inhabited, water is scarce and difficult to find in the dry season. But one creature that can always locate the most hidden springs and pools is the baboon. The Bushmen trick baboons into showing them where the water is by placing some chestnuts inside a hollow tree. The opening to this cache is barely large enough for the baboon to stick its paw in. When it reaches for the nuts and grabs a handful, the animal can't get its closed fist back out again. The baboon is too greedy to let go of the nuts, and so it is trapped. Hours go by, and eventually the baboon is too thirsty to stay. It lets go of the nuts and immediately runs to find water, with the lurking Bushmen following. The baboon has become their unwitting guide.

The baboon was freed when he changed his focus from the nuts to the water.

There's a moral here: As long as we are holding on to one particular thought, we are trapped in the cycle of negative emotions the thought is causing. To win the freedom you need, *focus on something else or on the positive side.*

TRAFFIC JAM

As in many cities, the traffic congestion on my way to work and home is very bad. It adds two wasted hours to my schedule every day. Instead of feeling upset or angry, though, I learned to use these two hours as my private time. I use them to do many things that I usually do not have time to do:

1. Listen to interesting interviews on the radio.
2. Listen to my preferred music.
3. Recite my prayers and gratitudes.
4. Do self-talk, self-analysis, and self-development.
5. Listen to audio courses.
6. Speak to my friends on the phone.

Well, I started enjoying the ride!

WORST-CASE-SCENARIO VISUALIZATION

Visualize a worst-case scenario and start exercising positive thinking by building new plans for the day.

COMMUNICATE

I will ask for clarification to understand a situation, and the opposite is true; I will communicate clearly the reason for my behavior. Clarity can shift almost any situation from negative to positive.

When I was reading about the paradigm-shift effect in Stephen Covey's book *The 7 Habits of Highly Effective People*, I decided to do a small experiment.

A week before Christmas, each person at work was selected to be an anonymous guardian angel of another colleague. As the guardian angel for a colleague, I bought a small teddy bear with a broken eye. It had been on the shelf of a shop for maybe three years, and on top of having only one eye, it looked old and used. Any person who received such a prank gift would not be pleased at all, I reckoned, and the first thing he or she would do would be to put that teddy bear in the trash.

Inside the wrapped gift, I attached a small letter addressed to the person, as if written by the teddy bear:

Please hear me before you make any decision.

Yes, I am blind, but it was not my fault. True, I am ugly, but I have a good heart.

As I was rushing to get out of the box and climb the shop's shelves, someone pushed me down, and I lost an eye.

Since that day, I've wondered who would come and take me home because, as you know, I was created to be with children who cherish me and love me.

As Christmas is on the way, I was praying and praying that someone, maybe as blind as me, would take me from the shelf and give me a warm home.

My dream came true, and today a man came to me and took the first step by getting me off the shelf—now it is up to me to do the rest.

I know deep down in my soul that you have a good heart, too, and you always think of helping others. So I am asking you to show me your kindness and generosity.

Please do not be ashamed of my face. Just look into my heart.

The teddy bear became a hero. Colleagues were talking about it, and it was a gift full of emotions.

The moral of the story is that we can shift the way we see things in many ways. Putting an emphasis on understanding and being understood, through love and care, is a good place to start.

Communication

I n Ron Deal's book *The Remarriage Checkup: Tools to Help Your Marriage Last a Lifetime*, there is a study based on fifty thousand couples' profiles.

The couples were grouped by five types, status of happiness, and the level of satisfaction was measured on a scale of 1–9 in eight subjects: communication, conflict resolution, finance, leisure, sexuality, family and friends, role sharing, and spiritual beliefs.

The group names and their descriptions and scores follow:

DEVITALIZED

The Devitalized group felt *extremely unhappy*, 79 percent of the couples considered divorce, and 69 percent did divorce.

The group level-of-satisfaction scores follow: communication 1, conflict resolution 1, finance 1.5, leisure 2, sexuality 2, family and friends 2, role sharing 4, and spiritual beliefs 3.

CONFLICTED

The Conflicted group felt *unhappy*, 73 percent of the couples considered divorce, and 53 percent did divorce.

The group level-of-satisfaction scores follow: communication 1, conflict resolution 1.5, finance 3, leisure 3, sexuality 3, family and friends 3, role sharing 6, and spiritual beliefs 5.5.

CONVENTIONAL

The Conventional group felt *happy*, 37 percent of the couples considered divorce, but this group had the lowest rate of divorce.

The group level-of-satisfaction scores follow: communication 3.5, conflict resolution 4, finance 4.5, leisure 5, sexuality 5, family and friends 5, role sharing 5.5, and spiritual beliefs 7.5.

HARMONIOUS

The Harmonious group felt *very happy*, 28 percent of the couples considered divorce, and the rate of actual divorce is unknown.

The group level-of-satisfaction scores follow: communication 5, conflict resolution 5, finance 5.5, leisure 5.5, sexuality 6.5, family and friends 5.5, role sharing 6, and spiritual beliefs 6.5.

VITALIZED

The Vitalized group felt *extremely happy*, 14 percent of the couples considered divorce, and the rate of divorce is unknown.

The group level-of-satisfaction scores follow: communication 7.5, conflict resolution 7.5, finance 7, leisure 7, sexuality 8, family and friends 7, role sharing 6.5, and spiritual beliefs 8.5.

If we look at the scores, even when the role sharing and the spiritual beliefs were high, couples were not happy because the other area levels of their life were not adequate due to *the low level of communication*. In relationships, having great beliefs and living by values is not enough to make the marriage or the relationship vital; communication is key. With good communication, you can affect all the other areas.

If we look at the extremely happy couples, the level of communication is almost the highest score; therefore, when you have high communication skills and spiritual beliefs that are in sync, you're doing really well in your relationship.

I have heard the word "communicate" thousands of times. You may think it would be easy to advise someone and tell him or her to communicate. Well, it is not. Effective communication is actually very hard. The way you communicate might hurt the other person, might result in a fight, or might lead to more conflict. These things can be so painful that we tend to avoid it altogether.

How can you communicate in a relationship when you don't have good verbal skills, when you don't understand the behavior of the other person, or when it seems that this person is using a different language?

To help you learn to communicate better, I have selected two areas to consider that will increase your communication skills at work and in relationships: gender intelligence and emotional intelligence.

GENDER INTELLIGENCE

The first thing people in an intimate relationship do is think of how they can change behaviors in their partner that they don't really understand.

Let me give you a few examples of this behavior that I've seen:

- I could not figure out why my wife got more upset when I tried to calm her down.
- I didn't know why she kept asking me if I loved her.
- She made me feel inadequate every time she stood in front of her closet saying she had nothing to wear.
- When she wanted to tell me a story, she would use so many boring details that sometimes I couldn't follow the story anymore.
- She made a big deal out of something that didn't seem important.

My wife and I have been married for thirty years. I am used to these behaviors and have accepted them, but I always wished she could change them. Two years ago, I read the book *Men Are from Mars, Women Are from Venus* by John Gray. At that time, I was giving seminars on happiness and emotional intelligence, and the book came as a revelation to me. I found out that my wife behaves like most women and that most couples' problems are caused by a misunderstanding of the way our genders are "wired."

When I shared the information on the gender differences in the book, I found out she also had wished to make changes to some of my behaviors, including:

- Why I didn't like to talk about my problems. It seemed that I didn't trust her.
- When she asked me, "What are you thinking about?" and "Nothing" was my reply.
- Why when she would tell me something, it sometimes seemed like I didn't hear her or care about what she was saying.
- Why I rushed her every time we wanted to go out.

She now knows that most men share those same behaviors.

In life as well as in relationships, we tend to give what we actually would love to receive, and we treat others as we would like to be treated. But in Mars-Venus relationships, you actually need to treat others as *they would like to be treated*. This is where gender intelligence makes the whole difference.

According to John Gray, men and women have different needs and, therefore, behave differently. Let me introduce you to few of these differences:

Venusians' needs: care, understanding, respect
Martians' needs: trust, acceptance, appreciation

All of us need all of these things to some degree. Repeatedly, however, these are the top three needs that come up consistently for women and the top three needs that come up consistently for men.

We've talked about the behavior cycle in the previous chapter; let us see now in Mars-Venus language how some behavior cycles work.

SHE NEEDS TO FEEL CARED FOR; HE NEEDS TRUST

When a man is interested in the woman's feelings and well-being, she feels loved and cared for.

When she feels loved and cared for, she becomes receptive and opens up to him.

When a woman opens up to a man, he feels trusted.

SHE NEEDS UNDERSTANDING; HE NEEDS ACCEPTANCE

When a man listens to a woman without judgment and with empathy, she feels heard and understood.

When she feels heard and understood, she will not try to change him.

When a woman tries not to change a man, he feels accepted.

SHE NEEDS RESPECT; HE NEEDS APPRECIATION

When a man acknowledges a woman's rights, wishes, and needs, she feels respected.

When she feels respected, she will show appreciation.

When she shows her appreciation to a man, he feels appreciated.

Men and women behave differently in communicating, processing information, leading, managing time, buying items, and coping with stress.

As you can see, gender intelligence is must-know information for every person. We all have the other gender in our life—in romantic relationships, in families, as friends or colleagues, and as business partners or clients. John Gray's series of books, will help you to find out what you need to know about the gender behaviors and differences in dating, parenting, working, and starting over.

I was so impressed by the way the gender differences empowered couples to better communicate and live a great marriage that I joined the Mars-Venus coaching program and became one of their certified life coaches myself.

EMOTIONAL INTELLIGENCE

Many subjects discussed in emotional-intelligence books and workshops have been shared in earlier chapters of this book. Because of the importance of this type of intelligence for communication-skills improvement, however, I will list the subjects that it addresses as a whole.

I suggest that you read two books by Daniel Goleman—*Social Intelligence* and *Working with Emotional Intelligence*. These will help you understand this seemingly soft skill's importance.

Much has been discovered in the past thirty years about emotional intelligence, and countless studies show the incredible role it plays in an individual's success. It has been shown that emotional intelligence, or EI, can be even more critical than the power of the cognitive brain—usually measured in terms of IQ. In others words, if you want to succeed, you would be much better off working on your soft skills—empathy, communication, understanding others, and so on—than on becoming better only at a specific technical skill.

These are the subjects that EI treats:

Self-Awareness: What is emotion? Why are we emotional? How does "emotional hijacking" take place? How does the brain process emotions? How does the brain perceive the world?

- What is a behavior cycle, and what are its implications? How can you boost your self-esteem? How can you analyze and balance life to make sure nothing is neglected?

Self-Management: How do you take advantage of the power of optimism? How do you manage your anger effectively? How do you control your worries?

- How do you prevent "flooding?" What are "positive replacement" phrases, and how can they help you?
- How can it help you to improve your interactions with others?
- Why do we worry? How do you use positive mentality? How do you automate positive thinking?

Self-Motivation: How do you motivate yourself? How do you avoid apathy? How do you be creative?

- Why do you become afraid? What are different kinds of fears, and how do you handle them? How do you get out of your comfort zone?

Empathy: How do you have empathic communication with others? What is the physiology of empathic communication?

- What are "emotional reactions?" What is the root cause of reactions, and what does it mean to you? How do you seek and give support? What is the best strategy to handle other people's resistance to your growth?

Social Awareness: How do you have effective group interactions? How do you listen positively? What are the "negative listening types?" How do you raise your social awareness through listening?

- How can you build rapport? How do you react to people who express negative emotions, and what are the implications?

Relationship Management: What are the "six human heeds?" How do you recognize the needs and desires of others? How do you categorize people based on their needs to make useful conclusions on follow-up actions?

Social Intelligence: How do you communicate, and how can this communication fail?

- What is the role of social knowledge within EI?

Attention: How can you achieve mutual attention?

- What is the physiological and psychological significance of eye contact?
- How do you mirror others and establish rapport?
- What are the significant verbal and nonverbal areas you can focus on to encourage others to open up?
- How can you show presence and charisma? How can you use acting to show confidence?

FROM MARS-VENUS COACHING PROGRAM:
THE SELF-ASSESSMENT TEST
Try the exercise below. It is a self-assessment that will help you rate many parts of your life according to how satisfied you are:

Please rate yourself on a scale of 1 (low) to 10 (high) on the following:

- Communication
- Friendships
- Motivation, passion, enthusiasm
- Focus, goal setting
- Decision making, problem solving
- Managing change
- Self-development skills
- Carrier development and improvement
- Time management
- Work-life balance
- Leisure
- Finances
- Career
- Health

- Positive attitude
- Happiness
- Spiritual

In relationships with

- Friends
- Coworkers
- Spouse/significant other
- Other family

Reading books alone will not help you improve all the ratings you wish could be higher. Attending workshops and seminars, however, will help you practice the skills you need to forge deeper social relationships. You will be amazed at what you learn from the experiences and testimonies of others. You can also get a life coach to help you achieve what you want.

Part 4
Happiness Intelligence

Happiness Advantages

Besides feeling wonderful and making us look attractive, being happy affects our environment and our health. Here are some of the advantages that many studies have shown of finding relative happiness:

1. **Happy people work better with others and have better relations at work and in their social life. This translates into the following:**

    -   Better teamwork with your colleagues.
    -   Better employee relations if you're a manager.
    -   More satisfied customers if you're in a service job.
    -   Improved sales if you're a salesperson.
    -   Better family and friend relationships.
    -   More kindness and acceptance.

2. **Happy people have higher levels of productivity, perform better in leadership positions, and receive higher performance ratings and higher pay. This is because of the following:**

    -   Happy people are more creative.
    -   Happy people fix problems instead of complaining about them.
    -   Happy people have more energy.
    -   Happy people are more optimistic.
    -   Happy people are way more motivated.

3. Happy people have better health.

- Happy people live longer!

A happy person has a more active immune system than a negative person. Positive emotions also protect people against the ravages of aging.

Studies have shown that biological age mirrors psychological age. For example, if your chronological age is fifty and your psychological age is thirty-five, biologically you look forty, but if your chronological age is fifty and your psychological age is sixty, biologically you look sixty-eight. What is very important about this study is that it shows your biological age can begin to reverse when you improve your psychological age. So be happy now, and in no time you will start looking younger!

In my research about happiness, I've found a common assumption: happy people have the above-listed qualifications. As a happy person myself, I agree with that assumption, but why do happy people have almost all the *same* qualifications?

In my latest readings, I've discovered that feelings of happiness are generated by some of the brain's neurochemicals: *dopamine*, *endorphins*, *serotonin*, *oxytocin*, and *testosterone*. Some people call them the happiness chemicals. According to studies, these feel-good chemicals are released in limited bursts for a specific aim and are stimulated by certain behaviors.

Normally, when we find out what stimulates our happiness chemicals, we'll try to repeat it time after time.

For feelings of well-being and joy, a person must stimulate these chemicals as often as possible. When the level of one of these chemicals is below normal, a person will sense that something feels wrong.

What is really important, as you will find out in the next chapter, is the correlation between the factors that stimulate the happiness chemicals and the qualifications of a happy person. They are incredibly aligned.

23

The Happiness Hormones

When your brain releases one of the happiness chemicals, you feel good.

A post published by Christopher Bergland on November 29, 2012, in *The Athlete's Way* states:

> *Life in the human body is designed to be a blissful experience. Our evolutionary biology insures that everything necessary for our survival makes us feel good. All animals seek pleasure and avoid pain. Therefore, our brain has a wellspring of self-produced neurochemicals that turn the pursuits and struggles of life into pleasure and make us feel happy when we achieve them.*

DOPAMINE

Dopamine is responsible for reward-driven behavior and pleasure seeking.

It gives you the feeling of joy, anticipation, enthusiasm, excitement, and being full of energy.

Those happy feelings are stimulated in the following cases:

- When you set a goal
- When you take a step toward a goal
- When you invest effort in learning, preparing, discovering, planning, and exploring, and expect it to be rewarded
- When your efforts are rewarded
- When you achieve a long-term goal

When a reward is delayed, greater amounts of dopamine are released, thus energizing, focusing, motivating, and driving the pursuer harder.

ENDORPHINS
Endorphins cause a person to relax, produce feelings of attachment, and promote a sense of well-being.

These have analgesic properties and are produced during energetic physical effort, sexual intercourse, and orgasm.

Humans experience endorphins as excitement levels increase in the following cases:

- When pleasing, laughing, smiling, and crying
- When exercising
- When having a massage
- When concentrating on positive thoughts and applying gratitude

OXYTOCIN
Oxytocin is a hormone directly linked to human bonding, and it increases the feeling of trust and loyalty. Oxytocin is created from the action of attachment.

It lowers stress in women, but does not have the same effect in men.

It's considered the "love hormone." High levels of oxytocin have been correlated with romantic acts and attachment.

In women, oxytocin increases in the following cases:

- With trust and when the need for caring, understanding, respect, and support are being met
- When helping, caring, sharing, or befriending without expectations
- When nurturing self

Oxytocin, the love and nurturing hormone, reduces blood pressure, cortisol levels, and fear. It creates a feeling of attachment and increases maternal behavior and sexual interest.

Oxytocin decreases when a woman feels alone, ignored, unsupported, and unimportant.

TESTOSTERONE

Testosterone is the hormone of sexual desire; it's associated with lust in both men and women and conveys powerful antiaging effects.

Testosterone contributes to a man's sense of power and well-being.

Working outside the home raises men's testosterone levels. It plays a role in assertiveness and drives competitiveness, creativity, and intellect.

Men produce thirty times more testosterone than women, and the right level helps men cope with stress. Women at work generate testosterone, but, unlike in men, it does not reduce their stress level.

Men need to feel successful at providing for their partner's fulfillment. Her response of trust, acceptance, and appreciation counteracts the effect of stress by stimulating a healthy level of testosterone.

In both men and women, high levels of testosterone can produce an emotional insensitivity and empathic block and increase aggressiveness and indifference to the distress of others.

Taking part in testosterone-producing activities at work can diminish women's oxytocin levels.

Testosterone is stimulated by the following:

- The conventional male-dominated work environment: goal setting, competition, problem solving, accountability, risk, dominance, success, efficiency, urgency, money, results, projects, and power
- Success or the anticipation of success in a relationship
- Forgetting one's problems, even momentarily
- Going into a "man-cave"

A man's confidence in his abilities increases testosterone and lowers stress, whereas the lack of confidence reduces testosterone, which can become a source of depression.

SEROTONIN

The brain's serotonin system is responsible for mood and emotions. Boosting serotonin transmission decreases negativity and increases positive responses.

Serotonin can affect social behavior, appetite and digestion, sleep, memory, and sexual desire and function.

Serotonin flows when you feel important and self-confident. Sometimes people make bad choices just to get that nice serotonin feeling. And sometimes people give up on feeling important—that feels bad, too.

To increase serotonin:

- Challenge yourself regularly, and pursue things that reinforce a sense of purpose, meaning, and accomplishment.

The brain keeps seeking importance no matter how much you feel like taking on tasks that make you feel important, because serotonin feels good.

Stress reduces serotonin levels.

Most antidepressant medicines provide, through the blood, serotonin to the brain, but the problem is that when we provide these elements *for* the body, the body stops producing them itself, and this results in medication addiction.

CORTISOL (THE STRESS HORMONE)

Cortisol is a hormone that the body naturally produces whenever a person experiences a stressful situation such as anger, anxiety, or fear, or faces a difficult problem, including finances, traffic, or familial or parental difficulties.

Cortisol is useful in giving a boost of energy to the body alert system, when we are under attack: it's our fight-or-flight hormone.

What do you think happens when you are under long-term stress?

Cortisol is designed to stay in our body for a few minutes only. When we are under continuous stress, we have a continuous high level of cortisol, which has a negative impact on the body.

When under attack, the body directs all its energy to fight or flee. A curtailed supply of energy to the digestive system, for example, results in weight gain.

When cortisol is high, we only burn carbohydrates and sugar for energy, instead of combined sugar and fat. The result is that we desire more comfort food.

It is not enough that we are dealing with these stressful situations. The brain's serotonin system, responsible for mood and emotions, also reduces its level when we are under stress.

Women *use* serotonin twice as fast as men because they use the two sides of the brain at the same time and *produce* serotonin two times slower then men. That is why women tend to go through depression more than men.

Raising the level of testosterone in men and the level of oxytocin in women reduces stress and helps the serotonin level to give us the feeling of well-being and put us in a good mood.

So when men have their highest degree of stress during the work day, they're using up their testosterone, and they need time to regenerate it.

To summarize:

Dopamine elicits feelings of: joy, enthusiasm, excitement, energy
Dopamine is stimulated by seeking pleasure, when effort is invested toward achieving things, in setting goals, in pursuing career and relationships, and in learning and exploring.
Endorphins elicit feelings of: relaxation and attachment
Endorphins are stimulated by smiling, laughing, crying, and exercising, and when dwelling on positive thoughts and applying gratitude.
Oxytocin elicits feelings of: trust and loyalty
Oxytocin is stimulated in women by romance, sharing, and being cared for and being understood, respected, and trusted. Also by nurturing self.

Testosterone elicits feelings of: confidence, creativity, and well-being

Testosterone is stimulated in men by competition, problem solving, risk taking, dominance, money, and power. It is also stimulated by the anticipation of success at work and in a romantic relationship.

Serotonin elicits feelings of: positive mood and attitude, general well-being

Serotonin is stimulated when we feel important and self-confident, when we do the right thing, and contribute to a good purpose.

CONCLUSION

All the things that stimulate happiness hormones are the necessary elements of success in relationships, career, health, and life. The body is programmed to want to stimulate these elements frequently; when it becomes a habit, your happiness chemical levels remain consistently high—and you become a happy person overall.

On the contrary, if you don't stimulate the happiness hormones, you'll feel that something is wrong.

24

The Right Time

THE TRUTH IS, THERE'S NO BETTER TIME
TO BE HAPPY THAN RIGHT NOW.

We spend most of our time in search of happiness. Sometimes, we convince ourselves that, at the sentimental level, life will be better after we find our soul mate, or then when we get married, or then when we have a baby, and then another. At the comfort level, we tell ourselves life will be better when we have enough money, or then when we have a big house, or then when we get a nicer car, and so on. But the big question is: *when* will I be happy? Is it when I retire?

It seems that our lives are dedicated to the pursuit of happiness. But happiness is often confused with pleasure; to maximize our happiness, we tend to increase the frequency of our pleasurable experiences and move from one to another quickly. Pleasure is an event generated by external resources. The more of it you have, the more neutral and less pleasant it becomes by comparison. When you get something you want, of course, you are happy for a little while, but that satisfaction is soon followed by a feeling of emptiness, and you start to want something else. The more you get, the more you need in order to maintain your happiness. You end up being dependent on things outside of yourself to make you happy.

Martin Seligman's book *Authentic Happiness* shares the following:

People who get more good things in life would in general seem to be likely to be much happier than the less fortunate. Good things and high accomplishments, however, studies have shown, have astonishingly little power to raise happiness more than transiently:

- *In less than three months, major events (such as being fired or promoted) lose their impact on someone's happiness level.*
- *Wealth, which surely brings more possessions in its wake, has a surprisingly low correlation with happiness level. Rich people are, on average, only slightly happier than poor people.*
- *Real income has risen dramatically in the prosperous nations over the last half century, but the level of life satisfaction has been entirely flat in most wealthy nations.*
- *Physical attractiveness (which, like wealth, brings about any number of advantages) does not have much effect at all on happiness.*
- *Objective physical health, perhaps the most valuable of all resources, is barely correlated with happiness.*
- *People who value money more than goals are less satisfied with their income and with their lives as a whole.*

Also based on Dr. Martin Seligman's studies:

External circumstances account for no more than 8 to 15 percent of the variance in happiness and the very good news is that the inner world factors, which are more under your voluntary control, account for the 85 percent of the variance of happiness.

The moral is: Don't expect the outside world to produce lasting happiness.

Happiness is within you.

Happiness is internally generated when you learn how to activate your happy hormones and can maintain them at constant levels. Of course, you cannot help but be affected by the outer world, but it will not depend on it.

THE HAPPIEST OF PEOPLE DON'T NECESSARILY HAVE
THE BEST OF EVERYTHING; THEY JUST MAKE THE
MOST OF EVERYTHING THAT COMES THEIR WAY.

Once you have awakened to this truth, the way to a better, more successful life becomes crystal clear. Train your conscious mind to think thoughts of love, success, happiness, health, prosperity, giving, and caring and to weed out negativity, fear, and worry. Keep your conscious mind busy expecting from God what is best for you, and make sure the thoughts you habitually think are based upon what you want to see happen in your life.

Living happy every moment was a choice I made, and with the help of God, I have regained my authentic nature, which is the goodness within me.

I am happy when I apply virtues—they have become my strength and foundation.

I am happy every time I make someone smile.

I am happy when working, creating, exploring, learning, reading, and socializing.

I am happy when I say "I love you" and share emotions with others.

I am happy when I see flowers, birds, plants, trees, the sun, the sea, and the beauty all around me.

I am happy every time I eat. Can you imagine how many have worked for you to enjoy one plate of food? Think of the bread only— some have planted the wheat and others have operated the machines, cars, ships, bakeries, electricity, gas, and many other things just for you to have bread. When you eat, enjoy and praise God, and be thankful to all these people.

I am happy when I am in bed, in the shower, in the car, watching TV, listening to music, talking on the phone, using the elevator, and so on. I am enjoying human innovation. Two hundred years ago, none of these conveniences existed. How fortunate we are.

I am happy when praying to and thanking God.

I am extremely happy when I talk about God's love and care and about everything I have learned.

I hope this book will help you find your authentic happiness and give you the ability to take full advantage of what life has given you in a way that benefits you and makes you happy.

This inner recovery journey is about understanding and dealing with the *power of the unseen*:

- The power of Father-Son relationship with the Creator.
- The power of the law of attraction when activated by condensed positive intentions.
- The power of thoughts when governed by values.
- The power of happiness chemicals when stimulated toward success.

I would like to give it a name: *happiness intelligence.*

$$25$$

Change the World

We all know of the many problems facing the Earth and its people. And I believe that although most people would like to do something about it, they don't because they believe that what they do will not make any difference.

I say that every person *can* make a difference in changing the world to be a better place, just by starting with his or her own relationships: family, colleagues, community, and so on.

Buckminster Fuller was one of the greatest inventors and thinkers of the twentieth century. He wanted to know what rules God used in setting up this universe. He used the bee example to describe the true purpose of life (http://www.healthy-holistic-living.com/how-to-know-your-life-purpose.html):

> *It is possible that the honeybee has a life purpose. What would that life purpose be? To pollinate plants, to keep life on earth. We wouldn't exist if it wasn't for honeybees.*
>
> *But do you think the honeybee gets up each morning and says to herself that she has to cross-pollinate plants? No. She just has—what goal? To collect nectar to make honey.*
>
> *The purpose of life is the side effect. In the case of the honeybee, the side effect is what? The pollination of plants, and the maintenance of life on earth.*
>
> *So, it's just possible that pollinating plants is the bee's true purpose.*
>
> *Now, if the honeybee has a true purpose, who else do you think may have a true purpose in life? Human beings of course.*

The moral of this example is that while pursuing your needs, desires, and goals, the side effect of your thoughts—remember the power of your thoughts on the physical world—and the side effect of your actions—remember the cycle of behavior affecting the behaviors of others—can improve the quality of people's lives if based on virtues. You will be then contributing to the goodness bestowed upon us by our Creator.

We can affect people when leading by example.

We can forward knowledge.

We expect our children to be honest when we are.

We expect our children to use integrity when we do.

We expect our children to believe in long-term marriage when we live a happy marriage.

We expect our children not to use drugs when we provide them with security, care, and love.

We expect our children to embrace human differences when we do.

As a role model, we can influence our friends, families, and colleagues.

It is like dropping a stone into the water. Ripples go out. That is, there is a side effect to the main effect. And the side effect can be very large.

We are building the future; it is up to us to choose what future we want for our children.

Martin Seligman said,

The good life consists in deriving happiness by using your signature strengths every day in the main realm of living. The meaningful life adds one more component: using these same strengths to forward knowledge, power and goodness. A life that does that is pregnant with meaning and if God comes at the end, such a life is sacred.

Join me in sharing happiness knowledge. It can change the world, one person at a time.

Testimonials

From Scarlette Sidawi Diab:

I've known Marcel for almost fifteen years. A few years ago, he started spreading the knowledge of happiness around him. And this knowledge has deeply affected me.

I learned how to deal with my daily activities in a positive way.

I have experienced God's help every time I faced difficulties, when I started practicing asking and believing in my prayers.

I started accepting others better than before.

He helped me get the best attitude ever, and into the habit of smiling.

He has contagiously transmitted to me the love of spreading happiness and joy among all the people around me.

I am really impressed by his great personality.

Thanks, Marcel, for everything.

■ ■ ■

From Raymonde Habbaki Abou Diwan

An inspiring life experience, supported by the essence of many valuable references. A proof that, whatever condition you are in right now, all you need to do is put God at the center of your life; communicating with Him will change your heart, and you will find peace, happiness, and satisfaction. All your needs will be taken care of.

Thank you, Marcel, for sharing.

■ ■ ■

From Georges Wakim

I grew up in a Christian family, but at the age of nineteen and after my dad's death, I was separated from God by anger and misunderstanding. I lived emptiness. I found myself searching for purpose and meaning in people and also in myself. I became very consumed with what people thought of me and was living for the acceptance of the world.

After a bitter divorce, Marcel has put me back on the right track of faith, and helped me overcome my divorce. And ever since I accepted Jesus into my life, everything feels better. I feel more relaxed and positively fulfilled knowing that God is watching over me today, tomorrow, and forever. The emptiness is now filled up with the Holy Spirit, and the secret behind that is to accept God into your life as a Father and Savior. I am not perfect, and I still mess up, but God loves me despite my flaws and imperfections. God has never once left me.

"Fear not I am with you till the end of time."

Thank you, Marcel, and thank God.

■ ■ ■

From Claudia Khoury

Divorced for thirteen years, mother of two teenage boys, one of them with learning difficulties, and we all live with my old, sick parents. Through these thirteen years, with no university degree, I worked very hard to improve my capacities and finally got a good job with a good income but still hardly covering my family needs.

With all the mess, the stress, and the huge responsibilities and problems that I had to manage, in 2013, at the age of forty-three, I found myself as a cracked woman who almost forgot the meaning of happiness, hope, faith, and self-esteem.

That's when Marcel Borgi gave me the chance at life-coaching sessions. To be honest my first thought was, "nothing will ever change. I will always be struggling in this black hole with increasing problems and responsibilities." After approximately two weeks of coaching, this impression disappeared, replaced by a kind of inner peace sensation. Marcel helped me discover myself. At the first stage, I wasn't capable of answering the most common questions about what I love, my fears, my dreams, my hobbies…In the coaching process, I was taught how to pray, how to participate in chats with friends and family, how to believe in myself, how to share my feelings and thoughts with the ones I love, and so many other things that I used to find impossible to do until I tried.

Since then and until now, the new me is a woman who always searches for new targets. I have changed from a woman who always underestimated herself to a woman proud of raising two great children alone and of reaching managerial positions without a certificate. The truth is that since the coaching began, I've faced quite a few hard times and at many levels (children's behavior, parents, work, and personal life), and I am really satisfied with my new way of thinking, acting, and controlling situations. Moreover, my positive attitude is inspiring people around me, which has given me the courage to share with them my experience, pushing them to overcome their hard times.

Yes, most of the time, life is hard, but it is we who should have faith in God and keep our positive thinking. It is a circle: we think positive, we act positive, and we receive way more positivity back.

Life coaching didn't change my life and didn't solve or erase my problems; it changed me. I was the problem, and now the problem is solved.

■ ■ ■

From my son Ralph

As we all know, most human minds are directed by default to negativity due to the unexpected and the unknowns. Words cannot fully describe my tribute toward my dad, who in fact changed my thoughts in a positive way.

My dad discovered a few years ago and through experience that trusting God and building a relationship with Him through goodness and prayers institutes wealth, prosperity, and happiness to the family, and, in fact, it did. Yet in his mind there was something missing, something pushing him to share his happiness and positivity with the surroundings, the community, and why not? With the whole society…that's where it all started and will keep on going again and again.

I'm happy that I have gained from him positive thinking and faith in God, even when I'm passing through my daily worries, fatigues, and weaknesses.

I'm glad to say that, in turn, I'm spreading this positivity to my friends and colleagues.

Thank you, Dad. God bless you.

■ ■ ■

From my daughter, Cynthia

You have always been my role model and mentor, ever since I was a little girl!

Day after day, year after year, your positive energy, your humbleness, your love for life, your magic power of turning the impossible possible, and your faith moved me, motivated me, and inspired me to become a better person!

Now I spread positivity, kindness, laughter, and love—and all of this is because I learned from the best!

I thank God for your existence.

■ ■ ■

From my wife, Mireille

Thirty years of marriage, always happy and in love. Yes, Marcel has known the real happiness and has transmitted it to me and the children. How was that?

It's very simple: he has given his total confidence to God. He considers God as a Father, and he believes that, as a real Father, God will watch over His children even in the smallest details; therefore, Marcel has developed the habit of communicating his needs and gratifications to God, and his prayers are answered.

His belief has helped me remove my worries for my children and my anxiety toward the future and obtain inner peace, and, in turn, I am trying to help people around me feel the same way.

He has taught me to thank God in advance as a proof of my total confidence and trust in Him, which was very difficult to do in the beginning.

I am very happy, and my happiness is reflected through my smiling face and positive attitude. When asked for the secret behind that, I answer, "I have known the real joy because I love and I believe that I am part of God and God is part of me."

Thank you, God, for putting Marcel in my path, and thank you, Marcel, for being part of my life.

■ ■ ■

From my son Paolo

Being happy was one of the biggest challenges I have ever had. I want to thank my dad, for without him I wouldn't have learned that happiness is the key to everything.

I started being happy rather than pretending to be happy by turning negative into positive and by living simply and loving everyone around me.

You give happiness a definition. For me, happiness is giving without expecting anything in return, is seeing the beauty in every person, and is making people smile as much as possible.

I am really lucky to have such a father because I know that most people aren't able to have what I have. Therefore, I am grateful to share and spread happiness as much as possible. I would like to end my testimony with an Albert Schweitzer quote that reflected what happened with me: "Success is not the key to happiness; happiness is the key to success."

■ ■ ■

From Sara Bejjani

God is giving us many gifts, and for that we should thank Him every day.

It is so hard to describe in a few words all the things I've learned from Marcel's coaching, but what I can say is that I discovered the real faith in God, a faith that gave me a peace of mind and soul.

Marcel made me realize that "God's joy is indescribable when I'm happy, so He will do everything to make me even happier," and that helped me be in a unique and priceless love with God.

I learned how to let go of the fear that was constantly inside me and let myself be guided by God's plans…I was happy again without anxiety in expecting God to take care of my needs.

And when I did, my prayers were answered.

God has given me many gifts, and crossing Marcel's path was one of the best! Thank you!

■ ■ ■

From Adeline Rizkallah Rahme

Knowing Marcel for many years as a colleague, I have witnessed his "transformation and evolution." I have seen him live and promote happiness every day.

He taught me that it doesn't matter what kind of person you are right now—it is the person you want to be that matters the most—that sculpting your character is a long process but not an impossible one.

■ ■ ■

From Johnny Homsy

When Marcel invited me to the Coaching Happiness Toward Success two-day workshop, my first thoughts were, "Can happiness be taught? Two days just to talk about happiness?" I was reluctant, but I accepted the invitation because that little voice inside urged me to.

The cause of my happy feelings, when they happen, did not occur to me till later, when I realized that happiness resides in my daily activities.

I recognized after the review of Marcel's personal experience and the "How to Live Happy" materials that happiness is a gift from God given to the person who asks for it.

Happiness starts as a tiny sensation and grows endlessly, whereas sadness starts big till it's melted away by happiness.

The training started with "the positive feeling that we get when we smile." When I tried it, I felt good, and I have learned to keep on smiling. Smiling triggered an internal feeling of joy.

I discovered that my smile is contagious. It positively affected the people I met, giving them good feelings, and since then, my anger has diminished. Starting with my family, I initiated a different life perspective. I excluded destructive reactions and learned to live and enjoy the present.

I also discovered my happiness in helping others. What an incredible feeling of joy I felt when seeing someone smile after having the opportunity to help in lifting some of their burdens!

I decided to communicate my happiness experience to every person I meet. I went back to every word that Marcel said in our several meetings and made a road map of my life and implemented it in my daily activities to the extent that I started teaching it to others.

My meetings with friends, family, and others became more enjoyable, whatever the circumstances were. This happiness has helped my family grow efficiently in a parental environment where communication boundaries have been lifted. That helped me become a father, a friend, and a mentor at the same time. What a joy!

It is a great act to transfer happiness to others. Shared happiness multiplies. Happiness helps to increase self-confidence. It expels fear and anxiety from the heart. It helps to reduce stress and mental depression. It restores health.

To live happily is a decision that we make. We should not hesitate to make this step as a healthy, contagious attitude for the people who open up to it.

Opening your heart to happiness will help you see the blessings that God has conceived for you in ways that you can never imagine.

Transformation

To express how I feel, I would like to use John's Gray words:

"I feel more and more that I am one with everything and everyone; my greatest joy is in serving. Life is a river of God's light and love gently rushing on toward more and more. I have become a pure channel of God's grace to all the people I meet."

I can briefly describe the transformation that happened to me as follows:

1. I asked God for help.
2. To feel I deserve that help, I try to be a better person to please Him.
3. When I started pleasing Him by being a better person, the pleasure became mine.
4. My pleasures became success, love, giving, and contributing.
5. Loving, giving, and contributing became helping God.

Happiness intelligence is, in fact, finding God within you, and with Him the impossible becomes possible.

Gibran Khalil Gibran, from *The Prophet*
"There are those who give with joy, and that joy is their reward."
"When you love you should not say, 'God is in my heart,' but rather, 'I am in the heart of God.'"

Benefits of Writing This Book

I have enjoyed every moment of writing this book. It revived my memory about my behaviors and beliefs and their effects on my life. I wondered how my life would have been "if I'd known back then what I know now."

Talking about the new me made me feel more grateful about how blessed and loved I am. We are all the precious children of God, and we are loved unconditionally and without exception.

Without this book, I wouldn't have known how much impact my coaching has made. It has encouraged me to do more.

The book has given me the opportunity to tell everyone that to change the world to be a better place, you just need to be authentically happy and teach other people how to be happy as well.

It has helped me declare to many unbelievers that "permanent" happiness is possible.

To be happy every moment was a big challenge; faced by the difficult waves of life, I had to struggle alone to learn how to surf. I hope this book serves as your surfboard in the sea of life.

Contacting Marcel Borgi

For those people seeking to implement the power of the unseen in their personal life and in their organizations, please visit www.marcelborgi.com or send an e-mail to mb@marcelborgi.com.

Thoughts and stories from readers are welcome.

Bibliography

The Bible. https://net.bible.org.

Byrne, Rhonda. *The Magic.* London: Simon & Schuster, 2012.

Chopra, Deepak. *Ageless Body, Timeless Mind.* New York: Harmony Books, 1994.

Chopra, Deepak. *Reinventing the Body, Resurrecting the Soul.* New York: Harmony Books, 2009.

Collins, Francis. *The Language of God.* London: Pocket Books, 2007.

Covey, Stephen. *The 7 Habits of Highly Effective People.* New York: Simon & Schuster, 1989.

Deal, Ron L. and David H. Olson. *The Remarriage Checkup: Tools to Help Your Marriage Last a Lifetime.* Minnesota: Bethany House Publishers, 2010.

Goleman, Daniel. *Working with Emotional Intelligence.* London: Bloomsbury Publishing, 1999.

Gray, John. *How to Get What You Want and Want What You Have.* New York: HarperCollins Publishers, 1999.

Gray, John. *Men Are from Mars, Women Are from Venus.* New York: HarperCollins Publishers, 2012.

Hawkins David. *Power vs. Force.* New York: Hay House, 2002.

Proctor, Bob. *You Were Born Rich.* McGraths Hill: Life Success Pacific Rim, 2003.

Redfield, James. *The Celestine Prophecy*. New York: Grand Central Publishing, 1997.

Robbins, Anthony. *Awaken the Giant Within*. New York: Simon & Schuster, 2003.

Seligman, Martin. *Authentic Happiness*. New York: Simon & Schuster, 2002.

Sharma, Robin. *The Monk Who Sold His Ferrari*. New York: HarperCollins Publishers, 1997.

Warren, Rick. *The Purpose Driven Life*. Michigan: Zondervan, 2002.

53361510R00127

Made in the USA
Lexington, KY
01 July 2016